Diving & Snorkelling Guide to

THAILAND

Frank Schneider

Consultant: Lawson Wood

jb

JOHN BEAUFOY PUBLISHING

At a Glance

Key to symbols

★   *location of site*
🚤   *duration of dive tour*
✪   *depth of dives*
👁   *visibility*
↻   *strength of current*
⭐   *special features*
▣   *skill level required*

Contents

Diving and Travelling in Thailand

An Introduction to Thailand

The Kingdom of Thailand is located in the heart of South-East Asia, bordered by Myanmar, Laos, Cambodia and Malaysia. The current king, who has been on the throne since 1946, is better known by his first name, Bhumibol. His name is spelled many ways: Bumiphol, Phumiphol, etc. This is because the phonetic spelling of the Thai alphabet can't be transferred into our alphabet according to fixed rules. It also means that the Thai word for 'island', for example, is sometimes written as Koh (with an h) and sometimes as Ko (without an h).

Thailand, formerly known as Siam

Until 1939 the country was called Siam, and in 1944 the writer Margaret Landon dedicated a literary monument to it in the form of the novel *Anna and the King of Siam*. The book was based on the memoirs of the Englishwoman Anne Leonowens, who worked as a nanny at the nineteenth-century court of King Rama IV (Mongkut). Siam gained cult status in 1956 with *The King and I*, an Oscar-winning film adaptation of the story starring Deborah Kerr and Yul Brynner.

The modern name Thailand comes from the Thai people, who, from around the year AD 1000, began migrating into the kingdom of the Mon and the Khmer States, which had already been in existence for two millennia. Although the Burmese destroyed the former capital of Ayutthaya in 1767, at the end of the day Siam knew how to stand up for itself. Thanks to the diplomatic skills of Rama IV, Thailand was never colonized, even during the era of European imperialism.

Since the military coup of 1938 and the name change from Siam to Thailand, instituted by Marshal Pibulsonggram (Phibunsongkhram) in 1939, the country has been on something of a political rollercoaster ride. Thailand's recent history of military dictatorships includes no fewer than 18 national coups interspersed with periods of democracy. Following a successful coup in 2006, and a less successful coup attempt in 2010, Thailand is now recognized as a constitutional monarchy.

An emerging country

Thailand is currently considered to be an 'emerging country'. It is no longer classified as a developing country, but has still to reach

Opposite Modern Thailand has retained the traditions of old Siam.

the economic level of a modern industrialized state (whatever that may mean, as they say with a wink in Thailand). By contrast, product piracy flourishes, and tourists will frequently be offered copies of high-price branded products, of variable quality. You should be on your guard against this counterfeiting, and remember that a fake Rolex watch or pair of Gucci glasses is likely to be confiscated at customs on your return home. You will not get your money back, and indeed you may even find yourself having to pay a heavy fine.

Open-minded kings

In the mid nineteenth century, King Rama IV ended the cultural isolation of Siam and set his country firmly on a course towards close political and economic relations with the Western world. During the reign of his brother, whom he succeeded, he was a Buddhist monk, and during this time he learned to speak English as well as studying French, Latin and medicine – he was very much a cosmopolitan man. As king, he introduced English in schools, and even established the handshake as a socially accepted greeting. His descendant, King Bhumibol, is equally revered and loved by his people. Respect for the royal family is deeply ingrained in Thailand. With this in mind, you should, for example, be careful not to step on the nation's currency, whether deliberately or accidentally. It is a punishable offence, because baht notes feature a picture of the king.

The king and the royal family enjoy the unconditional love and reverence of the Thai people.

You can take a helicopter tour of Phuket and marvel at the big statue of Buddha.
Photo: Skydance Helicopters Phuket

Religion

Ninety-four per cent of the Thai population is Buddhist, a small proportion is Christian, and there are also a few Hindus and Muslims. There is only one person in Thailand who is revered as much as the king, and that is Siddharta, the founder of Buddhism. Buddha is everywhere in Thailand. Every little village has its own temple complex, and the bigger a city the more impressive its temples. Incense permeates the buildings, and when you hear monks intoning their prayers during meditation, the exotic world of ancient Siam is almost within reach.

Getting there

Today, Thailand can be reached easily and comfortably. There are flights to Phuket or Bangkok from most major airports within about 11 hours. As always, prices often depend on the season. Check the internet for information on airports, destinations and prices. A passport is required for entry to Thailand, and on departure a tax of 500 baht is payable (with some airlines, this sum is included in the cost of the flight).

Following pages Time to relax on one of the many beautiful tropical beaches; the distinctive rock formation called Khao Tapoo or Nail Island.

Useful Facts

Currency: *Baht (1 pound = about 50 Baht; 1 dollar = about 30 Baht).*
Cash: *In tourist centres and in Bangkok, you can obtain money from ATMs using a European bank card.*
Medical care: *Clinics in Phuket are on a par with those in Europe. The island of Koh Lanta has European-standard medical care and a small emergency clinic.*
Immunisations: *None required. Recommended: standard immunization against tetanus, diphtheria, pertussis (whooping cough) as well as polio, mumps, measles, rubella (MMR) and influenza. Hepatitis A and typhus for long-term stays or special exposure, as well as hepatitis B, rabies and Japanese encephalitis.*
Eating and drinking: *Small food stalls or mobile motorcycle kitchens are the most inexpensive solutions. Even in holiday centres such as Khao Lak you can get a complete meal with drinks for the equivalent of less than £1 in the smaller local restaurants. Food in hotels, on the other hand, is mostly overpriced.*
Transportation: *Fast scooters can be rented everywhere. However, each year, many tourists have fatal accidents due to not wearing a helmet or riding under the influence of alcohol. Even if you are an experienced biker, the traffic situation in Thailand is anything but totally safe.*
Be careful when it comes to drugs: *Anyone found with drugs can face extreme penalties. Do not expect leniency. Offenders face the possibility of long-term prison sentences, and for more serious violations, such as drug dealing, even the death penalty may be applied.*

The Tsunami

Whatever else may be remembered in the long history of this tradition-conscious kingdom, whether historical events or legends, nobody in Thailand will ever forget what happened on 26 December 2004. It is a day that is forever engraved in the collective consciousness of modern Thailand.

It was a fateful day, caused by an earthquake deep under the sea. The tsunami that followed killed around 54,000 people in Thailand alone.

In Khao Lak and the neighbouring region of Bang Niang, the wave reached the beach at around 10:33 a.m. A wall of water, several metres high, struck the flat coastal area with such force that palm trees were uprooted and countless houses collapsed to the ground, without warning. Even substantial buildings went down like houses of cards.

Memorial in Bang Niang

Debris, trees and cars were swept inland in three consecutive waves. A police patrol boat ended up about a kilometre from the beach, across the main street, only coming to rest in the trees. It was subsequently turned into a tsunami memorial.

'People who look at the boat from the main street today can hardly imagine how everything was under water from here up to

The tsunami raged bringing untold damage and destruction.
Photo: W. Woerner

Ships were swept into the middle of Baan Nam Kem – hundreds of metres from the sea.

the edge of the forest,' comments Ernst Schläpfer, who runs the IQ Dive base in Khao Lak. He survived the tsunami, along with his whole family. 'I was lucky,' he says pensively. 'All we lost was our house.'

Jürgen Schenker and Benno Brandon of Dive Asia on the island of Phuket did not notice the disaster at first, because their diving school is located on a hill in the middle of the island. 'Since the tsunami, we all take more care of our family, friends and acquaintances,' says Schenker, who, like Ernst Schläpfer, is married to a Thai woman and has a son. Holger Schwab, head of Sea Bees Diving in Chalong, says, 'Strange as this may sound, in south-east Phuket people didn't notice anything at first.'

Rapid reconstruction

A year after the calamity, the infrastructure of Thailand's resort areas had been fully restored. Fears that large corporations might build big hotels and destroy the character of the place, particularly in Khao Lak or Bang Niang, have fortunately not been realized. Khao Lak and the island of Phuket have regained their long-established status as popular destinations.

Fact File

One year after the tsunami, Ernst Schläpfer found his dive computer under dried mud in the foundations of his house. He returned it to the manufacturer and had the data downloaded. On 26.12.2004, the device shows a dive from the time of 10:33. Duration: 27 minutes; maximum depth: 5 m; average depth; 3.1 m. The floor of the former house is about 5–6 m above normal sea level.

Safe diving in Thailand with DAN

Thailand is a wonderful holiday destination, with truly fantastic dive sites. However, for Europeans and North Americans it is not simply 'on our doorstep'. And as carefully as certain dives are planned and carried out, the possibility of a diving accident cannot be entirely ruled out. All the more reason to be prepared for the worst.

One organization familiar with these circumstances, and which cares for diving-related medical problems worldwide, is DAN Europe. The abbreviation stands for Divers Alert Network. DAN Europe is a not-for-profit organization that is active internationally. It has an established reputation in medical care and in health and safety research in the field of sports diving.

DAN has offices throughout the Asia–Pacific region, including Thailand, providing expert assistance and training both to local people and to visitors.

Pressure chambers in Thailand

With its RCAPP (Recompression Chamber Assistance & Partnership Programme), DAN helps to ensure the safety of pressure-chamber facilities in Thailand.

Fact File

- *Over 400,000 divers are DAN members.*
- *DAN members receive the best diving insurance.*
- *DAN deals with more than 16,000 emergency calls every year.*
- *There are more than 180 DAN doctors, leading specialists in their respective countries, who are available 24 hours a day, 7 days a week to provide the necessary support.*
- *There are hundreds of pressure chambers in the DAN network. They are all selected according to criteria of safety and reliability.*
- *Scientists and researchers from prestigious universities work in cooperation with DAN to make diving safer.*

The aim of RCAPP is the provision of and partnership with pressure chamber facilities, addressing issues of equipment, training and emergency management, for the purpose of ensuring their availability, quality and security in times of need. DAN has established well over 100 pressure chambers worldwide, including in Thailand. The first pressure chamber facilities assessed with the RCAPP procedure were those in Koh Samui and in Phuket.

The pressure chamber in Phuket was commissioned in 1996, and was the first in southern Thailand to treat diving incidents. It was initially used to treat incidents all over Thailand, from the west coast to the east coast and from the Burmese border in the north down to the Malaysian border in the south. With the increase in diving and the attraction of the islands in the Gulf of Thailand, a second pressure chamber was opened in Koh Samui in April 2000, thus allowing for shorter distances between accident sites and competent medical assistance – minimizing that all-important time factor.

DAN is a non-commercial organization dedicated to safe diving.

There are pressure chambers on Koh Samui and Phuket.

The operators of the pressure chambers in Phuket and on Koh Samui are the SSS (Sub-Aquatic Safety Services) Network. The aim of this organization is to provide such services where they are most needed. It is often the case that pioneering work needs to be done in areas where there are no decompression chambers available. It is fitting that the SSS network was the first to seize the opportunity (in April 2001) and order a comprehensive risk assessment of its two facilities in Thailand. These first two reports on Thai institutions paved the way for all subsequent evaluations (approximately 135 to date).

The pressure chambers are open to sports divers in Thailand, and met the minimum requirements as early as 2001. They guarantee injured divers treatment that is safe, effective and immediate.

Since then, the pressure chambers and their peripheral facilities have steadily continued to improve. The number of pressure chambers in Thailand has continued to increase. The most popular diving areas have pressure chambers and diving first-aid

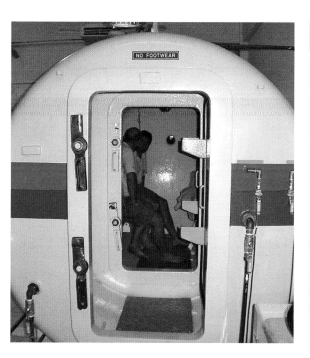

facilities, with the result that those who visit this beautiful underwater world will benefit from an invaluable service in the event of
an emergency.

Pressure chambers and medical centres for divers in Thailand:

· Phuket
· Koh Samui
· Koh Tao (*land-based oxygen treatment clinic, transfer
  to Koh Samui*)
· Khao Lak
· Krabi (*Medical Branch*)
  www.sssnetwork.com

Information and contacts

DAN Europe Foundation Website, *www.daneurope.org*
· DAN Asia-Pacific Website, *www.danasiapacific.com*

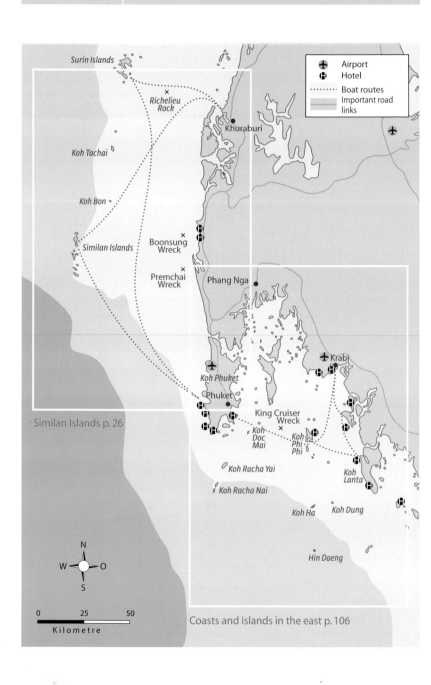

Surin Islands

Airport
Hotel
Boat routes
Important road links

× Richelieu Rock

● Khuraburi

Koh Tachai

Koh Bon

Similan Islands

× Boonsung Wreck

× Premchai Wreck

● Phang Nga

✈ Krabi

Koh Phuket

● Phuket

King Cruiser Wreck ×

Koh Doc Mai

Koh Phi Phi

Koh Racha Yai

Koh Lanta

Koh Racha Nai

Koh Ha   Koh Dung

Hin Daeng

Similan Islands p. 26

Coasts and islands in the east p. 106

N
W — O
S

0   25   50
K i l o m e t r e

Dive trips, liveaboards and more

Thailand has numerous dive sites for both beginners and experienced divers. With its mixture of corals and vegetated rocky reefs, it promises an attractive range of diving experiences, especially when you consider that many districts – for example, Richelieu Rock, Shark Point or Hin Daeng – are recognized as being among the best diving areas in Asia due to the abundance of fish.

Diving holidays on land and cruises
Thailand also offers the possibility of land-based diving holidays, staying in a hotel, and multi-day diving cruises. From Tap Lamu (Khao Lak harbour) cruise ships travel to the Similan Islands and the three northerly dive sites as well as to Surin Island. Chalong on Phuket offers multi-day trips to the southern sites, such as Hin Daeng, and to the Similan Islands.

Khao Lak and Phuket
Divers who find a week on a ship too much can travel from Khao Lak to the Similan Islands and the three northern sites – Richelieu Rock, Koh Tachai and Koh Bon – on day tours. The diving centres in Khao Lak also monitor the wrecks of two sunken dredger platforms. These former tin dredgers, which lie near the coast, are known as the Boonsung Wreck and the Premchai Wreck.

In and around Khao Lak, the land-based holidays are quieter than in the tourist centres of Phuket, such as Patong. On the island of Phuket, however, the atmosphere around Chalong is also very quiet, with a few small resorts that specialize in catering to

One notable diving cruise ship is the junk *June Hong Chian Lee* (www.thejunk.com).

divers. The diving centres in Phuket mostly use diving areas to the east and south-east of Chalong. Places like the Anemone Reef and Shark Point are among the best diving sites in Thailand and are best reached from Chalong, as is the wreck of the *King Cruiser*. There are other day tours that head from Chalong to other top diving sites in Phang Nga Bay.

Krabi/Ao Nang and Koh Lanta

The reefs around the islands near Ao Nang (about 12 in number) can be visited by long-tail boat, mostly during half-day tours. They are mostly simple dive sites that appeal to beginners or occasional divers. Dive sites around Phi Phi Island, the *King Cruiser* wreck or places like the Anemone Reef and Shark Point are further from here, and speedboats are needed to visit them.

Koh Lanta lies some 70 km south of Krabi on the eastern side of Phang Nga Bay. Most dive centres have their offices in Saladan, in the north of the island. From here you can reach Hin Daeng and Hin Muang on a day tour in three hours, in a large comfortable diving boat.

Opposite Seahorses can be seen at many dive sites in Thailand.

Useful Facts

- *Those who want to stay in small quiet resorts in Phuket will find a warm welcome, as will divers, in and around Chalong. If you are also looking for nightlife as part of your trip, the holiday locations along Phuket's west coast, or Ao Nang in the Krabi area, are recommended.*
- *In Khao Lak there are hotels of various categories and sizes, and beaches that are kilometres long — but no nightlife: the area is sound asleep by 11:00 p.m.*
- *Ao Nang in Krabi has developed into a lively resort. Here there are some luxury hotels, but inexpensive bed and breakfasts can also be found.*
- *Tourism in Koh Lanta is still in its early stages. Hotels and resorts in the various categories and price ranges provide all the amenities that you would expect from them, and there are long beaches along the west side of the island. However, unlike many other parts of Thailand, you will search in vain for nightlife.*
- *Almost all diving centres offer their guests transport to and from the hotel.*
- *If, having arrived in Thailand, you are only looking for an on-site diving centre, make sure that it is a member of a recognized sports diving organization (e.g. CMAS, Barracuda, PADI).*

The Similan Islands and the West Coast

A jewel in the Andaman Sea

The Similan Islands lie off the west coast of Thailand, in the Andaman Sea, exactly 61 km west of the resort of Khao Lak and about 100 km north-west of Patong on the island of Phuket. The Similan Islands are positioned along a rough north–south axis, covering a distance of just over 22 km. The geological origin of these granite islands lies in the Tertiary era, making them about 65 million years old.

The Similans were named by Malay seafarers. The word Similan is derived from the Malay word for the number nine (*sembilan*). The various islands now have Thai names, but diving instructors generally refer to them by number (1–9). Similan No. 1 is the southernmost, and No. 9 is the furthest north.

Since 1999, tourist activities have been banned on and around the three southernmost islands. One reason for this is to safeguard the spawning grounds of turtles on Similan No. 1, another is to protect the underwater world from all human influence. Outside the protected area, east of Island No. 2, which contains Boulder City, lies the southernmost dive site, while the Shark-fin Reef diving area lies south-east of Island No. 3. On Island No. 4, Koh Miang, there is an office responsible for monitoring the park. It also has some accommodation areas and two beautiful beaches that can be reached via a footpath. There is also fresh water on the island and, last but not least, the Thai Princess owns a holiday home here.

Koh Similan (Island No. 8) is the biggest of the group, with a surface area of approximately 13 sq km. It is here that the beach famous for its granite 'Donald Duck cliffs' is located. On No. 8 the park rangers have an office, and there are also a few accommodation possibilities here. Apart from No. 4 and No. 8, the Similan Islands are uninhabited.

Hard corals to the east of the islands

With approximately 25 different dive sites, this area is undoubtedly one of the best locations for diving in the whole of South-East Asia. The diving areas around the islands are well known for having two completely different characters. The reefs off the east coast are mostly hard coral. The reef surfaces here reach up to 3 m below sea level. From the edge, they more or less drop

Fact File

In 1982 the authorities designated the area around the Similan Islands and Koh Bon as the Mu Koh Similan National Park. It thus became the 43rd national park in Thailand. In 1998 the size of the protected area was expanded, with the inclusion of Koh Tachai, some distance to the north, to about 140 sq km. The islands themselves account for 15 sq km of this area, the remainder consisting of the protected marine zone. Fishing is prohibited.

Opposite The 'Donald Duck cliffs' on Island No. 8 – the symbol of the Similan Islands.

Leopard sharks are 'regulars' at the Similan Islands.

away sharply. Most of these reefs extend to an average height of 25–30 m from the sandy sea bed.

In contrast to the hard coral reef structures located along the east coast, the dive sites located on the north, south and west coasts are mostly large granite blocks with hard and soft corals and vegetation. They are generally a bit deeper, and are also more challenging.

Koh Bon, Koh Tachai and Richelieu Rock

Barely 25 km north-east of Island No. 9 lies the island of Koh Bon, with its small anchorage. Because of its relatively great distance from the Similan Islands, the Malay seafarers proclaimed the Similans to consist of nine rather than ten islands, not including Koh Bon. Nevertheless, the island is nowadays a part of the Similan National Park. Koh Bon is not just for divers – it also very popular with fishermen, given the excellent chances of encounters with big fish. In particular, there is a strong likelihood of seeing one or more mantas here.

Boats that run from Koh Bon head about 28 km north to stop at Koh Tachai. This island is often exposed to stronger currents that attract larger fish and other deep-sea dwellers.

About 43 km north-north-east of Koh Tachai lies Richelieu Rock, which projects barely 1 m from the surface of the sea at low tide. Richelieu Rock is also very frequently visited by deep-sea animals.

Impact of the tsunami on dive sites

The tsunami of December 2004 hit the Similan Islands as well as the mainland coast, but it did not have the same destructive force here. Near the islands it only caused an extreme rise and fall in the water level, together with unusually strong currents. These have had differing impacts on the underwater world of the diving areas, depending on the position of the reefs and the corals in relation to the direction of the waves.

Sometimes, between dives, there is time for a trip to the beach.

Next page This dive map shows diving sites around the Similan Islands and near Khao Lak, from Richelieu Rock in the north to the southern-most dive sites of the Similans and the two wrecks near Khao Lak.

Fact File

The Koh Tachai Islands and Richelieu Rock are the best dive sites for encounters with whale sharks.

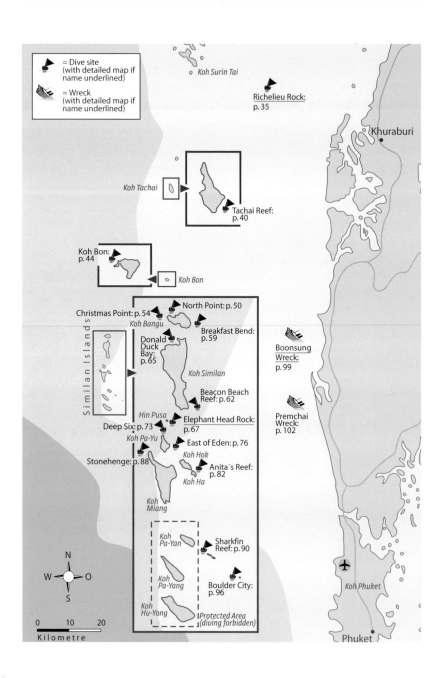

= Dive site
(with detailed map if
name underlined)

= Wreck
(with detailed map if
name underlined)

Koh Surin Tai

Richelieu Rock:
p. 35

Khuraburi

Koh Tachai

Tachai Reef:
p. 40

Koh Bon:
p. 44

Koh Bon

Christmas Point: p. 54

North Point: p. 50

Koh Bangu

Breakfast Bend:
p. 59

Donald
Duck
Bay:
p. 65

Boonsung
Wreck:
p. 99

Koh Similan

Similan Islands

Beacon Beach
Reef: p. 62

Hin Pusa

Elephant Head Rock:
p. 67

Premchai
Wreck:
p. 102

Deep Six: p. 73

Koh Pa-Yu

East of Eden: p. 76

Koh Hok

Stonehenge: p. 88

Anita´s Reef:
p. 82

Koh Ha

Koh
Miang

Koh
Pa-Yan

Sharkfin
Reef: p. 90

Koh
Pa-Yang

Boulder City:
p. 96

Koh Phuket

Koh
Hu-Yong

Protected Area
(diving forbidden)

Phuket

N
W O
S

0   10   20
Kilometre

In some places nothing has changed at all, but in other locations table and fan corals in particular were affected. As a result, after broken sea fans were gathered from some reefs and investigated by volunteers from the For Sea Foundation (*www. forseafoundation.org*), under the guidance of marine biologists, a number of corals have been reconstructed and/or fixed at specific locations.

Overall, the damage caused to the dive sites was estimated at 5 per cent – little damage – and significantly higher levels of damage were noted only in a few spots such as the deeper parts of Deep Six – 50 per cent of its structure was compromised. The marks mostly appear in shallower water, as well as at East of Eden, but this still counts among the top areas in the Similan Islands, as it has always done.

In the northern part of Breakfast Bend and North Point the tsunami was estimated to have left visible damage to around 15–20 per cent but caused no obvious destruction in the areas around Koh Bon, Koh Tachai or Richelieu Rock.

Diving and living
Khao Lak lies some 50 km north of Phuket Island, about an hour's drive from the airport. The resort and its neighbouring community of Bang Niang share a beach that is 1 km long. While there are some restaurants, and a few bars and souvenir shops, to be found along the streets of Khao Lak, Bang Niang is even quieter.

Fact File

In 2010 there was a prolonged increase in the water temperature (to above 30 degrees) in the Andaman Sea, and this resulted in some coral perishing (known as 'coral bleaching'). The worst affected areas included the Similan and the Surin Islands, but not all reefs were equally affected. It was mainly hard corals that were damaged (about 12–15 m). There was no visible damage to soft corals and sea fans. The Thai authorities closed some of the reefs in the Similan and Surin Islands. Of these sites, only East of Eden in the Similan Islands is notable. The current status can be followed on the Internet at www. tatnews.org.

The sandy beach of Khao Lak.

Previous page In place of massive hotels there are pretty resorts.

In both locations there are pretty hotels of various sizes and categories, and of course many diving centres. There were fears that, after the tsunami, the tourist resorts would 'colonize' the island, divide it amongst themselves and build big hotels – but fortunately this did not happen. The somewhat larger hotel Le Meridien, north of Bang Niang, has been around for longer.

From a tourism perspective, Khao Lak has not changed much in the few years since the tsunami. Compared to the bustling tourist centres along the west coast of Phuket, or at Ao Nang (Krabi), it is (as it has always been) much more comfortable, while the tourist resort of the still sleepy Koh Lanta Island is the best of the bunch.

Start in Tap Lamu

There are well over a dozen diving centres in Khao Lak and Bang Niang. All begin their trips in the small fishing port of Tap Lamu, about 12 km south of Khao Lak. There is a jetty here where big diving ships and long-tail boats are moored before they leave on trips to the wrecks. The journey from Khao Lak to Tap Lamu takes about 20 minutes; from Bang Niang it is about 30 minutes.

All diving centres begin their journeys in Tap Lamu.

Most of the centres in Khao Lak and Bang Niang, including the diving schools listed in these pages, have a pickup and delivery service from and to the various hotels in the area. If you want to borrow equipment on site, it is recommended that you make contact with them prior to your departure. That way you can be sure of having a suit of the right size, and that diving torches and underwater cameras will be available to rent.

Useful Information

IQ Dive
Ernst Schläpfer, the Swiss owner and manager of IQ Dive, has lived in Thailand since 1988 and is a Khao Lak pioneer. He has lived there since 1996, and even back then, when his was the only dive centre in the village, he offered daily trips to the Similan Islands. IQ Dive visits all of the diving locations in the region that are included in this book, some by speedboat. The centre is located on the main street in the middle of Khao Lak, opposite McDonalds.

IQ Dive also provides other forms of accommodation, such as the Ayara Villas on the beach in Bang Niang. Ernst Schläpfer and his wife Meaw also help in planning and organizing travel packages. The centre offers Nitrox for free, multi-day trips are provided, and it is open all year except July. *www.iq-dive.com.*

Sub Aqua in Khao Lak

The dive tour operator Sub Aqua established a competent partner relationship with IQ Dive in Khao Lak in 2008. The former Sub Aqua Khao Lak Dive Centre on the northern outskirts of Khao Lak, which was run by Wolly Woerner for a long time, no longer exists. Woerner, who has since passed away, had already initiated a collaboration with IQ Dive as early as 2005, after the tsunami. The European headquarters of Sub Aqua, in Munich, continues to maintain this cooperation.

Opposite, above The IQ Dive diving centre's boat.

Opposite, below The IQ Dive diving school on the main street of Khao Lak.

Below The Andaburi resort is situated on a hill on the north edge of Khao Lak.

The filling station shared between IQ Dive and Sub Aqua is located in the harbour of Tap Lamu.

Fact File

Off-season – There are diving centres that are fully active outside the main season, while others provide a reduced service. Those who still want to dive during the European summer months (the Thai rainy season) should contact the diving centre in advance, just to be sure. However, given that the weather can be very unstable at this time of year, it is quite possible that even a fully operational centre may have to cancel trips from time to time.

As far as the diving trips are concerned, in principle nothing has changed: these days, as before, all boat tours leave from the harbour in Tap Lamu, and the selection of diving locations remains the same. Nitrox 32 is available at no charge, multi-day trips are possible, and it is open all year round. *www.sub-aqua.com*.

Sea Bees Khao Lak

Many divers are familiar with the long-established diving centre in Chalong, Phuket, run by Holger Schwab. Since October 2005 there has been a branch in Bang Niang. As with the head office in Chalong, this Sea Bees centre has a hotel complex attached. In Khao Lak, the diving centre registration office and shop are located inside the new Palm Garden Resort. The hotel is located in the quiet countryside, just off the road between Bang Niang and Khao Lak.

Beginner divers are offered the opportunity of taking their first breaths underwater in the pool at the resort. Later on, there is a trip with a catamaran, which will serve as a dive platform. Nitrox and Tec dives possible, multi-days tours on offer, open from October to May. *www.sea-bees.com*.

Useful Facts

In Khao Lak there are several restaurants along the main street offering Thai and sometimes international cuisine. In most cases they are notably cheaper than the hotel restaurants. The excellent small local restaurant next to the IQ Dive centre is very characteristic of the country and extremely inexpensive.

One particular place of interest is the Takieng restaurant in Bang Niang, right next to the lookout point by the stranded police boat. The owner, Mr Wichai, has had his restaurant completely rebuilt in the wake of the tsunami. The north Thai 'Takieng' cuisine is 'à la bonheur' and worth more than a single visit. The prices here are also very reasonable.

The evening meeting place for divers and music lovers alike is the Happy Snapper Bar, situated in the upper beach town of Khao Lak.

Sea Bees Khao Lak offers not just a small, cosy hotel resort (**above**), but also a modern catamaran which takes divers to the most popular dive sites (**below**).

Richelieu Rock

A rock which is barely visible above the water at low tide marks one of the most legendary diving areas in Thailand – if not in the whole of Asia. Richelieu Rock, which is part of the Surin Islands Marine National Park, is located about 93 km north of the Similan Islands. For a long time it could only be reached during a diving cruise, but for a number of years it has also been possible to visit this site from the harbour in Tap Lamu, Khao Lak, on a day trip.

Opposite Dancing shrimps are generally found in colonies.

Following double page Soft corals love plankton-rich currents.

Richelieu Rock

30m
25m
30m
(24m)
29m
20m
20m
8m
(4m)
20m
10m (5m)
10m
10m
Small Channel
(19m)
12m
16m
12m
(12m)
30m
26m
28m
Sand
20m
30m
(12m)
30m
Sand

● Soft coral
∴ Anemone

At a Glance

★ 93 km north-east of Similan No. 9, 200 km north of Phuket, 80 km north-north-west of Khao Lak

⛴ multi-day diving cruises, whole-day tours with a speedboat from Khao Lak

✹ 5–35 m

👁 5–40 m

↻ weak to extremely strong currents

🐟 very good diving area for whale sharks

▣ for intermediate to experienced divers

By speedboat on calm water, the journey to the rock takes less than 2 hours. Cruise ships require 4–5 hours to get here from the Similans, depending on the state of the sea. However, many cruise ships arrange the journey to and from Richelieu Rock in stages – taking advantage of the fact that, in addition to the islands of Koh Bon and Koh Tachai, there are other dive sites between the Similan Islands and Richelieu Rock.

Richelieu Rock lies just 15 km east of the Surin Islands at a remote location in the open sea. There is an excellent chance of seeing big fish such as whale sharks, mantas, eagle rays, reef sharks and leopard sharks on most occasions. However, in rough waters, there is no protected place where boats can anchor; they must wait a safe distance from their divers with the engine running. However, while underwater, divers will find plenty of calm areas (as well as turbulent regions). Experience has shown that the best time for encountering whale sharks is between February and April.

The underwater landscape at Richelieu Rock appears as a crescent-shaped rock formation. The visible peak above the water is part of the largest contiguous block within the diving area. From the sea bed (about 20 m deep) one of its peaks, which rises west of the visible tip, reaches to 8 m below the surface; south-east of this is a crag that is only 5 m deep; and not far from this there is another, this time 12 m deep. On both slopes of the curved main block are two further formations at a depth of up to 12 m. To the west, a 28 m deep rock marks the extent of the rocky semicircle. Within the curve, to the east, there is a channel in the 20 m deep sand bed between the single and the opposite main rocks. The buoy line is also anchored near here.

Fact File

Richelieu Rock is without doubt one of the top dive sites in the world. The diving area is full of life great and small – plentiful molluscs and crustaceans, reef fish and larger fish.

All across the rock, there are narrow crevices and caves that provide shelter for smaller marine creatures such as ghost pipefish, banded and harlequin shrimps, toadfish and seahorses. In many places the rocks themselves are thickly covered with hard, horn and soft corals as well as many different kinds of sponge. Sometimes you get the impression that you are floating in a flower garden. There are shoals of fish that flit about, including snappers, glassy sweepers and fusiliers, while the open waters are patrolled by barracuda and other deep-water dwellers.

Although Richelieu Rock enjoys a reputation as a place to see whale sharks, the shark most commonly seen here is almost

At Richelieu Rock, marine life can be seen in all its colourful glory.

certainly the leopard shark. These animals are mostly found dozing on beds of sand. If divers observe them quietly and do not approach from behind, it is possible to get to within a few metres of them.

Safety Tips

With the 30 m diving depths and the state of the sea at the foot of the rock formations, decompression may need to be performed quickly. Decompression dives should be performed here only while the sea is calm, and each diver should be equipped with a surface marker buoy (SMB).

Koh Tachai

At a Glance

★ *about 20 km
north-north-west
of Koh Bon, 165 km
north of Phuket, 65
km north-north-west
of Khao Lak*
🚤 *multi-day diving
cruises, day trips
from Khao Lak*
⊗ *5–25 m (Leopard
shark Reef), 12–40 m
(Twin Peaks)*
👁 *5 –40 m*
⟳ *weak to
extremely strong
currents*
🐟 *very good dive
site for large sharks,
mantas, eagle rays
and barracuda*
📖 *for intermediate
to experienced divers*

At a distance of about 65 km from Khao Lak, the journey by speed-boat takes 90–100 minutes in good weather. Koh Tachai shows up as a green, overgrown rocky outcrop, with a narrow spur to the north. There is a beautiful and inviting beach on the east side, but this is only accessible at high tide. Close to the coastline, which runs in a relatively straight line obliquely from the east to the south, lies the Leopard Shark Reef. Another diving area, around 500 m south of the island, is the Tachai Pinnacle, which is also referred to as Twin Peaks by diving centres.

Because of its isolation, Koh Tachai is a habitat for many large fish, and a good place to encounter them. In the reef zones off the island, there is abundant life around the rocks, which are covered in hard and soft corals – everything from nudibranchs ('sea slugs') to large predatory fish. The fauna is enriched by exotic species such as toadfish and sea snakes. There are schools of blue fusiliers, sweetlips, the almost obligatory barracuda and fast swimmers such as mackerel, so you can be sure of seeing a lot of movement in the water.

Leopard Shark Reef dive site

Napoleon wrasse, schools of barracuda and the ever-present leopard sharks – that just about sums up the reefs on the east side of the island. They are located in shallow water with a depth of 5 m, about 30 m out facing away from the shore. This zone is parallel to the coastline and is lined with boulders and, in particular,

Leopard sharks are bottom dwellers.

Fact File

Along with Richelieu Rock, Koh Tachai is the best place for encountering whale sharks. At the Twin Peaks, there is also a good chance of seeing mantas and other rays, as well as the relatively common leopard sharks and occasional turtles.

Ornate ghost pipefish females are bigger than males.

hard corals. Brain, staghorn and fire corals are the most common here, but corals are scarce in those places where the reef runs out to the south in the deeper zones.

Leopard sharks are rarely seen in the shallow regions – they are mostly found dozing on the sand in the outer, deeper zone. In the reef you can see boxfish, lionfish, parrotfish and surgeonfish as well as occasional cuttlefish. Lobsters and shrimps are also numbered among the reef's inhabitants, as are moray eels and nudibranchs, and with a bit of luck you may also spot a ghost pipefish.

This dive site is also suitable for night diving.

Safety Tips

Very strong currents can occur around Koh Tachai. At the Twin Peaks, in particular, they can be so extreme that even diving with a mooring or buoy line can be extremely difficult. Always pay attention to the instructions of the dive guides!

Koh Tachai lies halfway between the Similan Islands and the Richelieu Rock.

Twin Peaks dive site

There are two rock outcrops sticking out of the water 300 m south of Koh Tachai, barely 50 m apart – hence the name of this dive site. It is marked by many buoys. The sea bed on the outer edge of the overall rock formation is about 30 m deep and falls away gently as the distance from Twin Peaks increases. To the south there are depths of 45 m. Between the two rock formations, the sea is some 25 m deep.

The northern part is made up of fewer blocks than the southern. The highest point lies to the north, 18 m beneath the surface. This area is covered in fan corals and different kinds of hard and soft corals.

The southern portion of Twin Peaks is rockier than its counterpart to the north. The highest point comes in the form of a flattened, coral-covered hill, which reaches up to 12 m from the sea bed. An additional peak in the area reaches 15 m high. The rocks on this edge have minimum depths of about 16–20 m.

To the west of the southern main block are about half a dozen other bigger boulders, scattered in a slight curve. At two different formations you can dive through a canyon to the other side. At the

The best time for observing whale sharks is between February and April.

eastern end there are many more smaller pieces of rock, most of them covered with various corals.

Leopard sharks like hanging around the sandy foothills, and toadfish are often found near small rocky niches or between corals. Even experienced divers sometimes startle the well-camouflaged toadfish as they swim past. In open water, you may be lucky enough to see a manta. Common batfish are frequently seen here, as are barracuda. Another possibility at this dive site is an encounter with a black-tip or white-tip reef shark.

Koh Bon

As far as the Malay seafarers were concerned, there were only nine Similan Islands. Nonetheless, along with Koh Tachai, Koh Bon is now part of the Similan Islands National Park.

Koh Bon is about 3 hours from Tap Lamu harbour by normal dive boat, and about 75 minutes by speedboat. On the south-west side rise green granite cliffs, which protect the anchorage cove from heavy seas and high winds. Koh Bon is popular among divers because of the good chance of encounters with big fish, but not only for that reason. Around the sloping rock saddle to the west, and just beyond it, there are good prospects of seeing one or more mantas.

In the anchorage on the south side of the west branch of the granite island, you should dive along the rock wall 'shoulder to the right'. The underwater world here is not particularly spectacular – the small and large coral blocks (often brain corals) are not the main attraction of the location, even though you can see snappers, grunts and fusiliers. However, this spot is the perfect place from which to descend to the area where the mantas are found. This is located in the foothills of the rocky underwater ridge in west Koh Bon where the overgrown granite, covered with small soft corals, falls away from a depth of 30–40 m. Those who reach

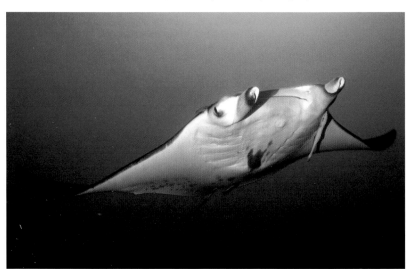

The protected anchorage of Koh Bon.

the underwater tip of the western point have the best chance of encountering one or more mantas above the rock and watching them float just below the surface. However, divers run the risk of being swept away by particularly strong currents in this area. There is not a lot of space, and not many rocks to cling to. It is safer and more convenient to watch the giant rays outside the turbulent areas. Some fish also swim close to the ground in dense

Opposite The name 'Manta Point' is appropriate.

Following double page Some nudibranchs are particularly colourful.

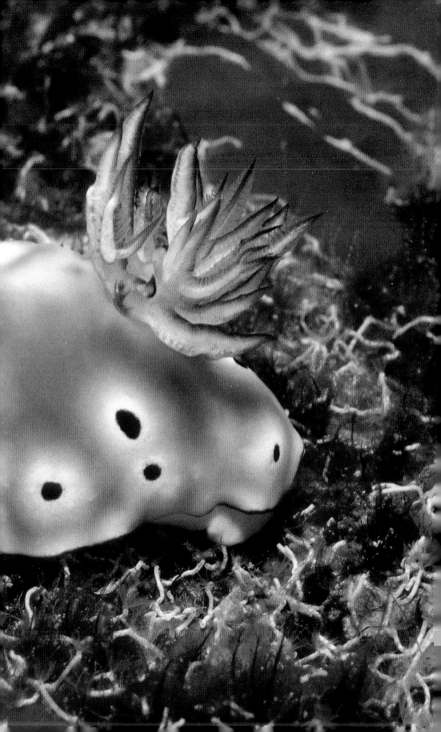

Corals feed on the plankton carried by the current.

Safety Tips

It is recommended to use a surface marker buoy when diving in current off the western tip of Koh Bon.

shoals. The reason for the frequent visits of the manta rays may be that this is a ray cleaning station.

Apart from the mantas, you may also come across leopard sharks in this area. However, they mostly like lying in the sand at greater depths, at the foot of the outward-sloping cliffs, where they sleep. Rare, but not impossible, are encounters with black-tip or grey reef sharks.

North of the underwater rock on the western tip there is a big coral block, at a depth of about 18 m. This is inhabited by nudibranchs and toadfish.

Shrimps can be found in shady crevices.

Deep dives should always be planned with caution, bearing in mind the sometimes extremely strong currents around Koh Bon. Decompression dives should be carefully planned, and should be undertaken only by experienced divers at times when there are no currents. Otherwise, the dive should be cancelled.

At a Glance

★ *off the north coast of Similan No. 9 (Koh Bangu)*
⛴ *multi-day diving cruises, whole-day tours from Khao Lak*
✪ *5–35 m*
👁 *10–40 m*
↻ *occasionally very strong currents*
🪸 *rocks have formed two channels which run parallel to the island*
🎫 *for experienced divers*

North Point (Rocky Point)

The name says it all – the northernmost dive site on Island No. 9 is also the northernmost dive site of the Similan archipelago. The gigantic granite rocks that characterize the underwater scene, and which make this dive site fairly typical of the Similan Islands, have also given it the name Rocky Point. However, most diving centres refer to it as North Point.

The sea bed around the rocks near the mooring line is about 20–25 m deep. Several granite blocks form tunnels. There is a canyon south of the mooring, whose base runs at a depth of about 17 m. Its direction is east–west, and it extends out to the southern flanks up to a few metres beneath the surface. Another channel runs parallel to this, further south, but this one is in shallower water and is less spectacular.

Camouflage: the bearded or tasselled scorpionfish is able to change colour to match its surroundings.

A porcelain crab on an anemone.

During the tsunami, many table corals and sea fans in the North Point area were damaged or destroyed. The For Sea Foundation re-established many corals, using complex techniques that included fixing fan corals with the aid of wires. More information is available on the internet at *www.forseafoundation.org*.

These days, North Point is still an attractive spot. South of the shallow canyon, at 10 m depth, it immediately borders a coral garden, which has grown up near the island and which runs along the shoreline. Staghorn corals in particular dominate the scene.

Above Around the rocks, shoals of fish like these attract sweepers.

Opposite Harlequin shrimps feed on starfish, cutting into them with sharp claws.

Close-up photographers and friends of nudibranchs, shrimps and ghost pipefish should take a careful look, for these popular small reef dwellers also live here. Turtle enthusiasts have a good chance of finding them at North Point too. The slightly deeper area of the dive site is regularly patrolled by leopard sharks, which like resting on the sand. You may also find stingrays, which cover themselves in sand and lie in wait. The blue water in the reef area attracts jacks, snappers and surgeonfish, and sometimes young barracuda.

At a Glance

★ *off the western tip of Similan No. 9 (Koh Bangu)*

⛴ *multi-day diving cruises, whole-day diving cruises from Khao Lak*

⊗ *5–35 m*

👁 *5–40 m*

↻ *some very strong currents*

➤ *west of the rock that rises out of the water is a big rock arch worth diving through; there is also a broad range of diving depths*

▣ *for experienced divers*

Christmas Point

Off the western tip of the northernmost Similan Island is a dive site known as Christmas Point where some large boulders have formed channels and tunnels. Two of these passages, at a depth of about 13 m, are very close to the boulder that breaks the surface of the water. You can get there by dropping a mooring buoy and anchoring the line at a depth of about 15 m, then diving to the south. West of here, at a depth of around 24 m, is an assortment of rocks where you can dive through an archway. Finally, on the outer western side of the rocks, in the Christmas Point area, it reaches a depth of 30 m.

This page This frogfish lies in wait for unsuspecting prey.

Opposite Banded shrimps are shy.

Following double page Frogfish are perfectly camouflaged on the reef.

If the currents, the availability of air and the conditions allow it, you can dive from the mooring to the deeper rocks to the west. You should then swim to the south, at a depth of around 25 m, to the granite rock with the archway. You climb gradually to the large central boulder and then head back to the mooring, either after you emerge or submerged at a moderate depth.

Along the coast, there is a coral garden at a depth of about 10 m, which consists of several sections of staghorn coral. The rocks at middle depth are partly overgrown with thick vegetation. There are also stately fan corals to be seen. The underwater landscape is home to nudibranchs, shrimps and angler fish, as well as angelfish, butterfly fish, boxfish and many glassy sweepers. There is also a scattering of cleaning stations.

Alongside the permanent reef dwellers such as moray eels, lionfish and various type of grunt, you can always encounter sharks at Christmas Point. As well as the commonly seen leopard sharks, you may spot white-tip reef sharks, especially in the deeper places. Encounters with mantas are also possible.

Safety Tips

Given the frequent strong currents, this is no place for beginners. There are several granite boulders offering shelter from currents, but you should avoid diving in the direction of the open water, so that you do not get carried away. Use a compass and a buoy!

Breakfast Bend/Snapper Alley/ Hideaway

The fringing reef south-east of Similan No. 9 goes by the name of Breakfast Bend. It stretches from the easternmost point of the island down to the southern tip, and extends just over 30 m from the shallow water zone to the sand. The diving area is formed for the most part of hard coral and drops off at an angle. However, the tsunami severely affected the corals here (the staghorn corals in

At a Glance

★ *off the south-east side and southern tip of Similan No. 9 (Koh Bangu)*

⛴ *multi-day diving cruises, whole-day tours from Khao Lak*

✖ *7–35 m*

👁 *15–35 m*

➲ *none to moderately weak currents*

➤ *easy diving, also very suitable for night diving runs*

▣ *for all experience levels*

This page The colours of the reef and its inhabitants are visible only with an underwater torch (or a camera flash).

Opposite The 'snapper route' lives up to its name.

Fact File

Because of the channel-like structure of the passage, the currents of the tsunami were particularly strong here. As a result, this dive site suffered more damage than others in December 2004.

particular) – in some areas it effectively destroyed large swathes of them.

In some places there are beautiful soft corals and sea fans, and, below the 20 m mark, the occasional black coral. Native to this area are trumpetfish, groupers, various types of grunt, a large range of butterfly fish and angelfish, and other colourful species. The coral stocks in the sand are overgrown with broccoli corals and partly covered by glassy sweepers. Bluefin trevallies, yellowsaddle goatfish and spangled emperors live here alongside medium-sized Napoleon wrasse.

The Snapper Alley dive site lies between Islands No. 8 and No. 9 at the southern tip of Island No. 9, a short distance from the tip of the fringing reef. Here, the underwater landscape is dominated by hard corals. This spot is also suitable for beginners and night diving runs. From twilight on, you can see the usual nocturnal animals, including lionfish.

After dark, you can find parrotfish woven into their sleeping cocoons. Crustaceans, such as lobsters, also come out of their hiding places at night – as do the animals that hunt them, including octopus.

This page This magnificent nudibranch goes by the scientific name *Glossodoris atromarginata*.

Opposite Lionfish are always vigilant.

At a Glance

★ *along the southern part of the east coast of Similan No. 8 (Koh Similan) as far as the southern tip*

🚢 *multi-day diving cruises, whole-day tours from Khao Lak*

⊗ *5–40 m*

👁 *10–30 m*

↺ *weak (sometimes strong) currents on the southern tip*

🐟 *large reef on the southern tip: there are frequent sightings of big fish*

▣ *for all experience levels*

Beacon Beach Reef

Approximately 200 m from the southern stretch of the east coast of Similan No. 8, a large reef extends from north to south, sometimes called Morning Edge or Beacon Point. It consists partly of hard corals, as well as huge rocks (predominantly in the south).

The biodiversity of the reef-building corals – found everywhere from the shallows to depths of over 35 m – is remarkably high. Gorgonian sea fans can be found in places in the deeper spots, as well as multicoloured, writhing whip corals. The coral site here was in fair condition after the tsunami.

Along with the coral, the reef's fauna is also highly diverse. In the shallower areas you can see anthias and other small reef fish. Mantis shrimps and eels live around the scattered clusters of hard coral. With a bit of luck, you will see nudibranchs, shrimps and rare crabs, lobsters, various types of anemonefish, several species of lionfish, batfish, many shoals of fish and larger solitary fish such as John's snapper along the reef, as well as titan triggerfish or adult eels. Turtles and sea snakes can also be found along the coast. In the deeper regions, stingrays can frequently be seen lying in the sand.

Big fish are mostly to be seen at the southernmost tip, known as Beacon Point. Here, the dive site is what is probably the largest granite rock of the Similan Islands. Its growth suffered a bit as a result of the tsunami, but, as in many other places, the damage is no longer obvious.

Io the north, the rocks get smaller as they head into the steeply sloping southern end of the Beacon Reef, which reaches the sand at a depth of 30 m.

Tuna, black-tip and grey reef sharks are not commonplace at Beacon Point, but they are seen now and again around the rocky southern slope of the reef. Eagle and manta rays are also occasionally seen here.

Fact File

The wreck of the liveaboard Atlantis X *dive ship lies approximately halfway along the reef, at a depth of 15 m (bow) to 30 m (stern). However, this ship, sunk in 2002, is only of interest to those new to wrecks.*

Opposite The mantis shrimp carries its eggs around with it.

Below Juvenile ribbon eels live in small burrows and under coral rubble.

Safety Tips

Both beginners and experts can dive in this spot, at their own risk. The reef is so big that multiple dives with different depth profiles can be made. However, so-called 'yo-yo diving' (continuously changing between a deep and shallow dive profile on the same dive) should be avoided. Caution: at Beacon Point, dives of more than 40 m are possible.

Right The banded sea krait is more poisonous than any snake on land – luckily it is not aggressive.

Opposite page Turtles often come into the bay to feed.

Donald Duck Bay

Donald Duck Bay is named after a rock which, seen from a certain angle and with a little imagination, is said to resemble the head of the cartoon duck. Below the rocks at the north end of this bay lies a small and simple dive destination, ideal for twilight and night dives. It stretches south of the visible rocks off the headland. Due to its sheltered position in the bay, there are usually no currents here – those that are present are very weak.

The sandy soil around the rocks is relatively flat and gradually reaches a depth of 20 m. It is marked by occasional small outcrops of hard coral; on the outer rocks there are also small soft corals and sea fans. Throughout the day there is a reasonable chance of encountering turtles.

During the night, lionfish swim through the light cones of the underwater lamps, hoping for prey – and this means that they often come very close to divers.

At a Glance

★ *northern foothills of the bay of Similan No. 8 (Koh Similan)*

⛴ *multi-day diving cruises, whole-day tours from Khao Lak*

⊗ *5–20 m*

👁 *5–30 m*

↻ *weak to no currents*

🐟 *ideal dive spot for twilight and night diving*

▣ *suitable for beginners*

Safety Tips

When diving you must pay attention to the shipping, especially if you move further into the bay, away from the rocks on the north side. The best way to alert approaching ships to your presence is with a surface marker buoy.

Shrimps shelter in the columns of rock and hard coral, as well as lobsters where there is room. Nudibranchs also occur in large numbers. Beneath overhangs you will find parrotfish beginning to spin their sleeping cocoons.

It is hardly worth diving in the bay itself, especially as there is always boat traffic in this area throughout the day.

The titan triggerfish is the most imposing of this fish family. During the spawning season it becomes very territorial and will attack anything (including divers!) if you get too close to the nesting site.

Elephant Head Rock

This dive site has two Thai names, Hin Pusar and Hin Hua Kalok. The latter means 'skull', and it is probably for this reason that this well-known dive site – often described as the most spectacular in the Similan Islands – acquired the name Elephant Head Rock.

Four granite rocks, three high and one somewhat lower, can be seen from afar. The largest of them lies to the west. Some rock formations reach up to 5 m below the surface of the water, but others only reach 26 m, even at their highest elevation. The lowest point of these low-lying rocks is 35 m deep. The slope drops steeply to about 30 m, especially on the west side of the big rock that rises out of the water.

To the west of the southernmost of the three big rocks, and in the midst of them, there is a canyon between two cliffs, about 22 m deep. The highest point of the southernmost rock reaches up to about 20 m. Its tip (which borders the rock that towers out of the water) is very popular with photographers. Many beautiful soft corals grow here, attracting plenty of animals.

The underwater landscape of the entire dive site is marked by

Following double page
Grunt frequently hide under table corals.

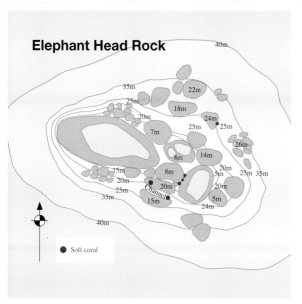

At a Glance

★ about 1.5 km north of Similan No. 7 (Koh Pa-Yu) and 1.5 km south of Similan No. 8 (Koh Similan)

🚢 multi-day diving cruises, whole-day tours from Khao Lak

✪ 5 m to more than 40 m

👁 10–40 m

🔄 weak to very strong currents

🚩 there are no mooring lines

📖 for experienced divers

Gorgonian sea fans stretch up towards the sun.

Safety Tips

Thanks to the way its boulders are positioned, Elephant Head Rock has some spots where you are protected from the current, even when it is strong. Nevertheless, the recommendations of the diving guides should be followed: in some places, turbulence can make for unpredictable conditions. The western side of the large rock drops down steeply, and this can result in a downward current under certain circumstances. In normal cases, it is not so strong as to pose a risk; generally you should just swim laterally out of the current. A buoy should be carried.

narrow passages, overhanging rocks and small caves. In many places there are passages that can be dived through, and these are among the highlights of the dive site. Depending on the current, divers must take care that they do not get pushed against the rocks and damage the corals.

While there are some granite rocks that are practically uncovered, sponges, soft corals and cup corals have settled on many other rocks. The latter are popular hiding places for small blennies and hawkfish. In addition, there also countless gorgonian sea fans.

Above The west side of the great rock falls away steeply.

Previous page, above Another spectacularly beautiful nudibranch – *Chromodoris geminus*.

Previous page, below Black-tip reef sharks are sometimes encountered at Elephant Head Rock.

In dark corners, you can find the endemic Andaman grunt, while white-tip reef sharks wait for the night beneath overhangs. The medium depths are inhabited by groupers, angelfish and a range of surgeonfish. When you go diving in the deeper regions, you may encounter mantis shrimps, fire gobies, sand perches and dragonets, while nudibranchs and nematodes live in the shallower areas. Barracuda of various sizes and black-tip reef sharks occasionally drift past the reef, and sometimes you may see mantas near the rocks. Even whale shark encounters are possible at Elephant Head Rock.

Deep Six

Like some other dive sites in the Similan Islands, Deep Six has more than one name – it is also known as Fanfare Point. This diving area is in effect an underwater extension of the northern tip of Island No. 7.

In general, the tsunami caused more serious damage on the west side. But there was also considerable damage to the east in places where there was nothing to stem the flow of the current. In some places, table corals were overturned and sea fans were broken, but the effects were not so dramatic in those areas where the Deep Six rocks blocked the current and protected the corals. A diver who did not know this corner of the reef before the tsunami would barely be able to tell that anything had happened. Overall, this dive site has lost none of its attractiveness.

As the name Deep Six suggests, the area around the rocky tip of Island No. 7 is suitable for deep diving trips. Here, there is a kind of Massif Central, which is an extension of Koh Pa-Yu. Some tunnels, which one can dive through, have been formed out of the arrangement of granite rocks of different sizes. These passages

At a Glance

★ *extension of the northern tip of Similan No. 7 (Koh Pa Yu)*

⛴ *multi-day diving cruises, whole-day tours from Khao Lak*

⊗ *5 m to over 40 m*

👁 *10–30 m*

↷ *weak to strong currents*

⚑ *Deep Six was affected by the tsunami on the east side, but in other places it has remained a beautiful dive site*

▣ *for intermediate to experienced divers*

The tips of a lionfish's fins are packed with poison, so take care when approaching them.

The big pufferfish has strong jaws.

are located at depths of between 10 and 23 m. The sandy bed around the big rock complex falls away from a depth of 10 m near the island, down to 30 m or more.

Between the granite rocks, which appear to descend into the depths like a giant staircase, you can find the endemic blue-spotted jawfish, amongst other marine life. Around the tunnel, the characteristic striped oriental sweetlips and the spotted harlequin sweetlips are commonly seen. At the western end of the reef,

Nudibranchs are quite a common sight.

Soft corals only spread their tentacles in the presence of a current.

there are beautiful fan corals (as always). Lionfish and butterfly fish reside there, and every so often a white-tip reef shark will pass through the reef. Bannerfish, red-toothed triggerfish and smaller schools of midnight snapper populate the scene. Around the rocks to the east of the dive site there are, along with pretty sea fans, small pink soft corals.

At a Glance

★ *along the southern part of the north-east side of Similan No. 7 (Koh Pa-Yu) and around the eastern flank towards the island's south coast*

⚓ *multi-day diving cruises, whole-day tours from Khao Lak*

⊗ *5–35 m*

👁 *10–40 m*

⤴ *weak to strong currents*

✈ *generally acknowledged as one of the top dive sites in the Similan Islands*

⚐ *mild to moderate*

The tiger cowrie (*Cypraea tigris*).

East of Eden

The dive site referred to as East of Eden by most diving centres is also known as Morning Edge. The reef stretches north of the east-ernmost point of Similan No. 7 right down to the southern tip of the island. The area as a whole is home to one of the most colour-ful and possibly the most beautiful underwater scenes of the Similan Islands. East of Eden is a perfect combination of hard and soft corals, all surrounded by white sand. In the middle section, some of the coral growth is rather less pronounced. However, the biodiversity is evident across the entire dive site.

Away from the coast of the island, the reef falls away steeply, reaching depths of 40 m or more. To the north, the deeper regi-ons (30 m) are supersaturated with bushy soft corals, fan corals and black corals. Between them romp countless types of fish and small organisms. Soldierfish hide in shady areas, bigeyes roam in a leisurely fashion through their territory and bluestripe snap-pers flit past in teeming shoals. Divers who like to look for smaller marine life may also come to this reef. Animals such as longnose hawkfish, fire gobies and ghost pipefish can also be seen here, as can nudibranchs and cowries.

Always moving through the reef: butterfly fish.

One of the best places in the reef is a coral block that rises from a depth of 22 m on the sandy bottom up to 12 m below the surface. It is located at the southern end of the eastern flank of Island No. 7 and is beautifully covered with soft and fan corals. Almost at the centre of the eastern flank, at a depth of only 15 m, can be found what are probably some of the biggest sea fans on the whole reef. In the light of underwater torches, they glow in a striking shade of orange, a beautiful contrast to the bright blue of the water.

Following double page
The trademark fan corals at the East of Eden dive site are remarkably large.

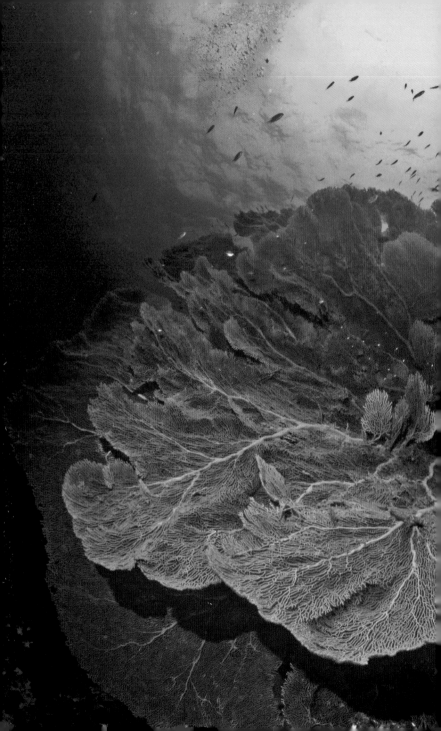

Fact File

East of Eden is considered to be one of the best places in the Similan Islands. It is always worth bringing an underwater camera. With a wide-angle lens, the various coral species offer abundant coloured motifs, and there are countless patterns at close range.

Above right   Seahorses are fond of fan corals.

Opposite page   The claws of a mantis shrimp can break the glass of a diver's mask.

Below   Bigeye soldierfish love dark hiding places.

Throughout the reef, particularly in the deeper regions, there is a chance of seeing white-tip or black-tip reef sharks, and of course there are often leopard sharks lying on the sand.

At a Glance

★ the reef runs east
of Similan No. 6 (Koh
Hok) to the south-
east, along the east
side of No. 5 (Koh Ha)
and around to the
south

⚓ multi-day diving
cruises, whole-day
tours by speedboat
from Khao Lak

⊗ 2–27 m

👁 10–35 m

↻ weak to
moderate currents

➤ diving depths
range from the
shallows down to
30 m or more

▣ suitable for
beginner divers

Anita's Reef

In some diving centres, Anita's Reef is also called Barracuda Point
or Morning Glory. Although the northern tip of this reef starts
around the east coast of the small Island No. 6, the greater part
of it runs along the south-east side of Island No. 5. Close inshore,
it is very shallow at first, before it gently falls away to a depth of
about 30 m. From a diving perspective, it is hardly worth going
deeper than 25 m.

There are some beautiful table corals to be found in the upper

Soft corals are related to sea
anemones.

areas. They often hide coral fish. In the deeper areas of the reef, the sea bed consists of bright coral sand. Scattered across the deeper regions of Anita's Reef are some large coral growths. They are covered with soft corals of bright red and purple, as well as crimson anemones.

The shy garden eels live in the sandy depths, retreating into the sand as soon as divers come within range. In this vast area, there is a good chance of encountering stingrays. These animals are normally harmless, even when observed from relatively close by. However, they should not be cornered by two divers approaching simultaneously from different directions, and they should never have their escape routes blocked, or they are likely to defend themselves with lightning quick twists and turns. A sting from one of these animals, while not necessarily fatal, almost always causes necrosis around the wound, and it will certainly be very painful for a long time.

Among the coral blocks, populated by jewel groupers and anthias, there are several cleaning stations. The area becomes significantly more rocky towards the southern tip of the island,

Fact File

Anita's Reef offers dive sites at various depths, and is therefore suitable for all divers no matter what their level of experience.

Stingrays are not normally aggressive.

Safety Tips

You should never approach a stingray if the sting at the end of its plate-shaped body is raised, even if the animal is in a resting position.

before descending to a rather steeply sloping hard coral reef.

One of the hallmarks of the reef is a large block of coral, which can be found south-east of Island No. 5 at a depth of 20 m, north of the mooring anchorage. Its highest point is around 12 m under the surface. It is covered with beautiful soft corals and big fan corals; the area is also populated by various hard corals.

In 2003, the Similan National Park administration sank a wreck to the south of island No. 5, thus creating an artificial reef. The 30 m long boat lies at a depth of about 40 m, tilted to one side with its highest point at approximately 30 m, so the average diving depth is normally more than 30 m. But Anita's Reef, with its corals and fish, promises significantly more attractive dives, so a visit to this so-called Tuna Wreck is not particularly recommended.

Following double page At Anita's Reef there is a wreck at around 40 m.

Opposite page A scorpion-fish lurks in a crevice.

Below Fish swarm across the reef.

Stonehenge

At a Glance

★   *about 67 km west of Khao Lak, about 90 km north-west of Phuket*
⚓ *multi-day diving cruises, whole-day tours from Khao Lak whole-day tours from Khao Lak*
⊗   *18–35 m*
👁   *10–30 m*
↻   *weak to strong currents*
➤   *dive site in open water with relatively great diving depth*
▣   *for intermediate to expert divers*

This dive site in open water, north-west of the tip of Island No. 4 (Koh Miang), is fairly deep. The sandy bed is around 30 m below the surface, with a number of huge boulders projecting from the sea bed, reminiscent of a megalithic stone circle. Hence the name of this place – from the famous stone circle at Stonehenge in England.

The shallowest point is at a depth of about 15–18 m. This results in an average diving depth that is always significantly greater, so it is essential to keep a constant eye on your air supply, dive time and decompression. The position of the dive site, between the islands, favours strong currents, but the great depths also improve your chances of encountering large fish.

Divers with limited experience should always be accompanied by an experienced guide.

Mantas can sometimes be seen around Island No. 4.

Above Bigeye soldierfish.

Among the fish that can usually be seen at Stonehenge is the small white-tip reef shark, easily identifiable by its flat head, Eagle rays and the rare guitarfish also appear on this reef from time to time. Hiding in the crevices you are likely to see several kinds of soldierfish and lionfish, as well as grunt, both singly and in groups. Large lobsters are best spotted by their long feelers, sticking out from their burrows like long antennae.

The underwater landscape is dominated by big, beautiful sea fans in their hues of ochre to bright orange, black corals and green tree corals as well as large barrel sponges. Sometimes, mantas can be seen in the open water, as well as fast predators such as tuna, barracuda and some species of mackerel, which also hunt along the reef in the deep water. In this area, ghost pipefish provide highlights and lively splashes of colour.

Safety Tips

Given its position and depth, dives in the Stonehenge area must be carefully planned, and must be executed in a disciplined manner.

Sharkfin Reef (Hin Phae)

At a Glance

★ approximately
1 km south-east of
Similan No. 3 (Koh
Pa-Yan)
⛴ multi-day diving
cruises, whole-day
tours from Khao Lak
⊗ 5–40 m
👁 10–30 m
↺ weak to strong
currents
➶ rocks that
stretch out
approximately 1 km,
straight from the
north-west to the
south-east
▣ for divers with
an intermediate level
of experience

The approach to Sharkfin Reef is almost identical to the approach to Boulder City except that it is just over 1 km further north-west in the direction of Island No. 3. In calm weather, you can see parts of the reef's granite boulders from the boat. Three rocky outcrops rise up from the middle section to just below the surface of the water. With a little imagination, these rocks look like the dorsal fins of sharks, which is how this dive site got its name.

In the northern part of Sharkfin Reef, beautiful sea fans grow next to hard and soft corals.

The reef stretches for almost 1 km, and its south side is characterized by relatively steep rock walls or slopes to the sea bed, which is about 20 m deep. But on its northern side Sharkfin Reef slants somewhat more precipitously. Here as well, the sandy bottom is about 20 m deep.

Like the rock, the sea bed on the north side also dips more gently, while in the south it drops into the deeper regions quite rapidly. It ultimately drops to 40 m or more around Sharkfin Reef. The direction of the current here is almost always at right angles to the reef, so that one side of the reef is sheltered from the current.

At Sharkfin Reef, the northern part is populated predominantly by hard corals and staghorn corals. There are also soft corals and beautiful fan corals. Most of these sea fans glow bright orange. The hard corals on the northern slope are frequented in part by shoals of sweepers.

In the northern part of the reef, the rocks in some places have formed tunnels. One of them (at a depth of approximately 14 m) is

Only half as beautiful without a diving light: in the spotlight, the glassy sweepers sparkle like pieces of gold.

Most fan corals here are orange.

not too far from the anchorage point of the mooring buoy, and it can be dived through relatively easily.

There are many blue-striped snappers and grunt in the passages. There are also large areas where the landscape is marked by green tree corals and sea fans. On the south side of the reef complex you can often see large schools of barracuda, forming huge circles and drifting, apparently aimlessly,

Safety Tips

In a strong current, one side of the reef offers protection from the current. Nevertheless, you should not head too far from the rock formation in the direction of open water. There, the current strengthens again and is capable of quickly carrying a diver far away, making a return to the reef difficult or even impossible.

Left Batfish usually circle a few metres below the surface.

Following double page Leopard sharks can also swim very quickly.

along the reef like a silvery windsock. White-tip reef sharks, found throughout the region and usually growing no larger than 1 m in length, occasionally lie in small caves, like bamboo sharks. Only rarely are they seen swimming around during the day. Turtles frequent the shallower regions, and further down, in the sand along the Sharkfin Reef, leopard sharks can often be seen.

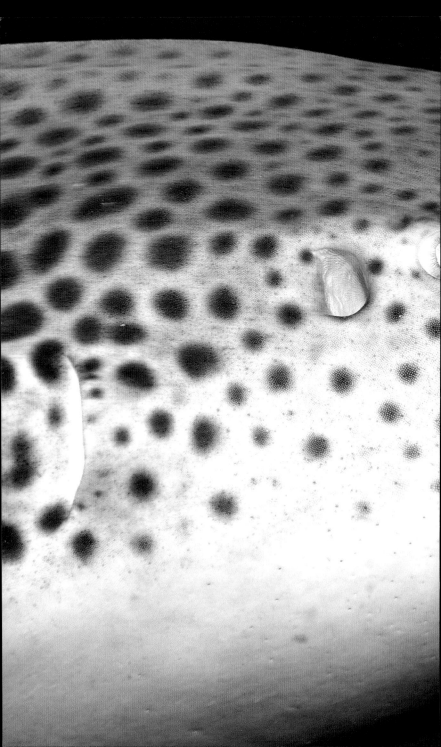

Boulder City

In calm weather, this dive site, some 60 km from the coast, can be reached by speedboat in a mere 90 minutes or so. In a normal diving vessel it takes about 3 hours.

Boulder City is the end of a gigantic rock outcrop running from the east side of Island No. 3 (Koh Pa-Yan) across the Sharkfin Reef before heading further to the south-east. From there, the rock formation runs into the sandy sea bed.

The name Boulder City is a fitting one, as there are a lot of

The real colour of the corals can only be seen with the aid of a torch.

Napoleon wrasse.

them, some of considerable size. The huge granite rocks, partly covered in colourful soft corals, green tree corals and sea fans, lie scattered in the sand. There are also pore and staghorn corals here and there.

Between the large and the medium-sized rocks, with a bit of luck you can spot big fish, such as roundhead parrotfish and Napoleon wrasse. In the deeper regions (25 and 30 m) leopard sharks are a common sight on the sandy bed. On the other hand, the small rays, although they are anything but rare, are not so easy to spot, since they camouflage themselves by covering their entire bodies with sand. If one of them is discovered, it will go to look for a new hiding place – and while it is doing this you can often watch how a ray digs through the sand by making fluttering movements with its body.

Boulder City is also one of the few places in the Similan Islands area that is home to Dory, the colourful surgeonfish that starred in the film *Finding Nemo*.

The largest rock formation of Boulder City lies at the north-ern end of the dive site. It reaches a depth of up to 16 m. At its westernmost point, the sea bed drops away another 30 m or so.

Turtles are excellent divers.

The scorpionfish sucks in its small fish prey and quickly tears it apart in its mouth, swallowing it immediately.

On the eastern side of the big rock lies a smaller granite rock, whose tallest point stretches up to 18 m.

When you dive from here a little further south over the neighbouring small rock, you reach the next biggest formation, which rises up to 12 m beneath the surface. Turtles and bigger fish, including groupers and Napoleon wrasse, like hanging around in this area. To the south, across a sandy bed that is not protected from the current, lies the third granite massif. Its highest point is 18 m. All in all, this makes Boulder City a relatively deep dive site.

When the current is strong, you should only dive around the central rocks, since these offer sufficient protection from the current. On the route over the sandy bed (25–30 m deep) to the southern rock formation, divers run the risk of being carried away by the strong currents.

Safety Tips

This is a relatively deep dive, and divers need to keep an eye not only on their air consumption but also on their dive and decompression times.

Boonsung Wreck

The name is somewhat misleading, because this dive site, located about a 30-minute boat ride from Tap Lamu, is not a ship but a former tin dredger, which was sunk in 1984. Before the tsunami it had a nearly rectangular layout and resembled a floating platform. The force of the wave split the metal construction into a number of pieces of different sizes.

The wreck, despite looking less than spectacular at first glance, is a really good dive site. It teems with fish, and you can occasionally see leopard sharks. With a bit of luck you'll even have an encounter with a whale shark. This spot is legendary for the winter of 2003/04, when six sightings of whale sharks were reported at the wreck site.

As has already been noted, the Boonsung Wreck is not a ship. It was in fact a rectangular support platform with storage space, but with no high superstructure. The tsunami divided the wreck into three to five (depending on how you count them) big sections, which lie only a few metres apart. The main axis of the wreckage still lies roughly in a north–south direction. On the west side, the large X-shaped bracing pattern is still visible on the outside wall of the wreck. This is the secret symbol of the Boonsung Wreck.

The wreck is regarded by countless animals as a replacement reef. In addition to numerous dense schools of fish, there is also an abundance of lionfish. Tropical scorpionfish, stonefish, moray eels, different types of nudibranchs, small shrimps and crabs –

Lionfish swim freely around the wreck.

Boonsung Wreck

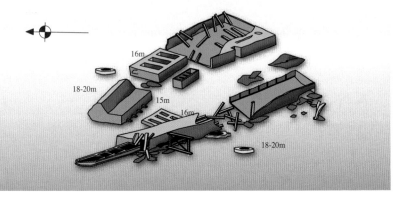

At a Glance

★ approximately 22 km north of Tap Lamu harbour and 13 km west of the coast, roughly level with Khao Lak; around 90 km north of Phuket

⛴ half-day tours from Khao Lak

⊗ 15–20 m

👁 5–25 m

↻ weak to strong currents

🐟 next to the Prem-chai Wreck; the only appreciable diving area in the coastal area around Khao Lak; unusually large numbers of fish

▣ suitable for beginners

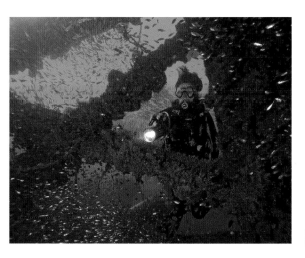

At the wreck there is an incredible abundance of fish.

the fauna is truly diverse. However, the undisputed favourites of the divers here are the leopard sharks, which can be encountered on most dives. The Boonsung Wreck may not be particularly big, but given the extraordinary abundance of fish it is easy to spend an hour-long dive here without getting bored. The dive should begin around the sandy bed and between the two main blocks of the wreck and should finish as you climb to the somewhat higher upper sides.

Safety Tips

After the tsunami, apparently inviting openings and crevices formed in many places across the wreck, but it is unwise to enter them. There is too much danger of metal parts breaking off or of the wreck caving in.

Opposite Almost every column in the wreck is inhabited by a moray eel.

The Boonsung Wreck is suitable for twilight and night dives.

Premchai Wreck

★ *some 12 km
south of Tap Lamu
in the coastal area
around 80 km north
of Phuket*

⚓ *half-day tours
from Khao Lak*

✖ *12–24 m*

👁 *5–25 m*

↩ *no current to
strong currents*

🐟 *aside from the
Boonsung Wreck this
is the only notable
dive site near the
coast of Khao Lak;
extraordinary
numbers of fish*

▣ *suitable for
beginners*

Since August 2001, the diving centres around Khao Lak have had an additional diving destination off the coast. The Premchai Wreck lies less than 30 minutes south of Tap Lamu. This is a former dredger – it is not a cargo ship, as is often claimed – that lies bottom-up on the sand bed, with storage areas for the salvaged tin. Unlike its counterpart to the north, the Boonsung Wreck, there isn't much to see. There is no noteworthy coral growth here, which means that you can also expect the Premchai Wreck to be rich with fish life.

As a half-day diving destination near the coast, the Premchai Wreck to the south of Khao Lak is a good addition to the more

Like the Boonsung Wreck, the Premchai Wreck was not a ship but a tin dredger.

Safety Tips

Going inside the wreck is not recommended, as the condition of the metal is now uncertain. There is a danger of pieces falling off, causing hazards or even completely blocking your route.

well-known Boonsung Wreck. This former dredger, while largely still intact, is barely covered due to its location. After the dredger sank, the sides were welded in some places as part of salvage operations. A complete view of the wreck is often not possible due to large numbers of plankton, so divers are sometimes unable to see it as a capsized vessel. However, you can see large shoals of certain kinds of fish here, like snappers and fusiliers; lionfish and scorpionfish hide in the niches and columns. Particularly conspicuous are the batfish that circle around the wreck in small groups, and leopard sharks that like sleeping on the sand bed (alone or in groups). In addition, yellowfin barracuda can be seen almost everywhere.

Above Visibility can fluctuate.

Left Batfish approach quite close to divers.

Coasts and Islands
in the East

Diving near Ao Nang, Phuket, Phi Phi and Koh Lanta

East of the southern part of Phuket and, to some extent to the south of the island, there are dive sites that can be reached on day tours. There are also dive centres on Phi Phi Island and Koh Lanta to the east, which run trips to these places. You will need to take into account the differing travel times that are needed to get to the various sites. The places with the longest journey times are the diving schools in Ao Nang and Krabi to the north (although there are also some local dive sites around the coast there).

In contrast to the Similan Islands and the west coast, most of the dive sites described here can be reached without the need for particularly long travel times. However, with the exception of local dive sites near Ao Nang, day trips are often the only thing on offer. In principle, dives take place right into the afternoon, even from Phuket or Koh Lanta. In Ao Nang, on the other hand, normal diving operations include half-day trips to the offshore island.

Islands near Ao Nang.

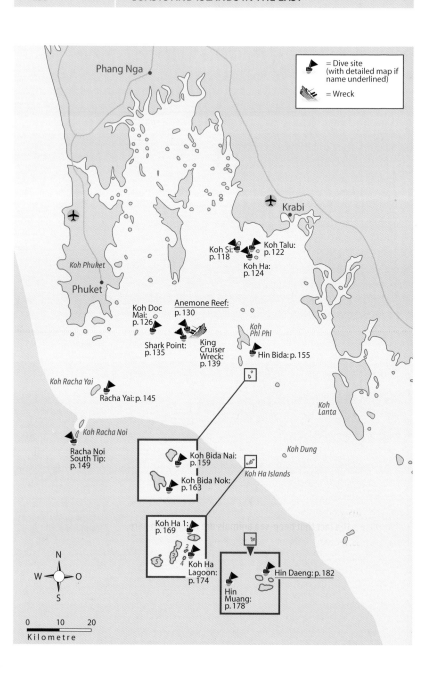

= Dive site
(with detailed map if
name underlined)

= Wreck

Phang Nga

Krabi

Koh Si:
p. 118

Koh Talu:
p. 122

Koh Ha:
p. 124

Koh Phuket

Phuket

Koh Doc
Mai:
p. 126

Anemone Reef:
p. 130

*Koh
Phi Phi*

Shark Point:
p. 135

King
Cruiser
Wreck:
p. 139

Hin Bida: p. 155

Koh Racha Yai

Racha Yai: p. 145

*Koh
Lanta*

Koh Racha Noi

Racha Noi
South Tip:
p. 149

Koh Dung

Koh Bida Nai:
p. 159

Koh Bida Nok:
p. 163

Koh Ha Islands

Koh Ha 1:
p. 169

Koh Ha
Lagoon:
p. 174

Hin Daeng: p. 182

N
W — O
S

Hin
Muang:
p. 178

0   10   20

Kilometre

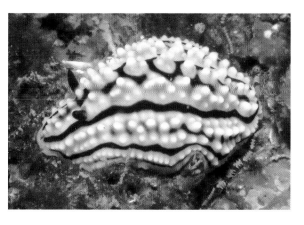

With warty nudibranchs, it is not always easy to tell which end is which. Here, the small feelers at the front of the animal can be seen to the left.

Ao Nang: relaxed diving

The coastal resort of Ao Nang in Krabi offers several hotels and, in addition to the many souvenir shops, plenty of diving schools, especially in the beach promenade area. This should come as no surprise, as a glance out to sea shows about a dozen islets. This is where the local dive sites are situated. In contrast to the districts in Phi Phi and Phuket, which run day tours to these places, it is a matter of a half-day trip to the nearby islands. Long-tail boats can reach these sites in under 45 minutes.

The dive sites around Ao Nang include simple beginners' dive sites as well as sites for all levels of experience – but this benefit is probably perceived by more experienced and demanding divers as a disadvantage. They will look in vain for steep walls extending to a depth of 30 m, or extensive reefs for drift dives. Around the islands, dives seldom go deeper than 15–20 m.

Even so, there are places like Koh Ha, with extremely attractive coral growths. And in the wider area there is plenty to see. This partly offsets the fact that deep-sea animals are rarely seen here. Nevertheless, leopard sharks are at home here, and even encounters with whale sharks should not be ruled out.

On land, Ao Nang, with its many souvenir shops, T-shirt shops, restaurants and bars, is very lively. There is a broad range of hotels on offer, from the luxurious Krabi Thai Village down to the bed & breakfast beach establishments. (Almost) everything is possible.

Fact File

On the whole, dive trips in the Ao Nang area are very relaxed. Those who want to include a few nice quiet dive runs in their holiday to Thailand are in the perfect place here.

Phuket: top spots for wrecks

Chalong Bay lies at the south-eastern corner of Phuket Island. It is the starting point for excursions to some of the best dive sites in the region. Anemone Reef and Shark Point are, in fact, just as interesting as the Similan Islands. With their strong coral growth, their large sponges and a stunning abundance of fish they are so impressive that some divers will certainly plan more than one descent in this area during their holiday. In addition, the sunken wreck of the *King Cruiser* ferry is located in this area. When the ship ran aground on the Anemone Reef in 1997, all the passengers were brought to safety in time. Incidentally, the boats from dive centres along the west coast of Phuket – Patong Beach, Kata, Karon or even further north – also anchor in Chalong Bay, close to the diving areas east of Phuket.

Compared to Phi Phi Island, where the tsunami of December 2004 claimed numerous lives, Chalong's coastal area and the local harbour were largely spared. The reason for this lies in the geography: Chalong is sheltered by its recessed position between two sloping shores. However, the old wooden pier, which could previously be accessed on foot (if only for a short distance), is now nothing but a memory. Fortunately, the modern dive boats had already started using a new pier before the tsunami. It stretches so far out to sea that guests are brought to their ships from the parking area in little buses.

As Anemone Reef, Shark Point and the *King Cruiser* wreck are all located close to each other, the diving centres have a highly diversified portfolio in their programme. You can basically experience everything here: from the small, rare frogfish, through to leopard sharks, up to whale shark sightings – anything is possible at these three dive sites.

Visibility varies in this part of the Andaman Sea. Sometimes visibility is 25–30 m, but at other times it may be reduced to a mere 5 m or less. While such extreme conditions occur only exceptionally, it is worth noting that conditions can change quickly. Murky water today does not necessarily mean that it will be the same tomorrow. From Phuket or Chalong, you can also dive at the sites near Phi Phi Island.

Opposite The *King Cruiser* sank in 1997.

Large grouper.

Koh Lanta: legendary places a stone's throw away

For a good few divers, the local ambience and the holiday resort atmosphere are important aspects to take into account when it comes to choosing accommodation. The nightlife in Saladan cannot compare with that of the west coast of Phuket, but those who enjoy peace and quiet should love Koh Lanta. Although there are luxury resorts to be found here (albeit fewer than elsewhere), this eastern island is regarded as relatively sleepy by tourist standards.

On the other hand, as far as diving is concerned, Koh Lanta is in the top league. The cliffs of the Koh Ha island group can be seen on the horizon off the west coast of Lanta. However, they have nothing to do with the similarly named spot near Ao Nang – neither in appearance nor under the water.

Most of the diving centres are located to the north, in the small resort of Saladan. It also has the largest selection of hotels in the region.

The Koh Ha rocks near Koh Lanta.

Koh Lanta can be reached from the mainland via two short transfers that only take a matter of minutes, and not far from the ferry terminal you will also find the departure point for diving boats. Diving from a long-tail boat plays no role in Koh Lanta – the areas that are visited by the big diving ships are too attractive and too diverse, and in one of these the journey to Koh Ha takes around 90 minutes.

The legendary sites of Hin Daeng and Hin Muang are, quite justifiably, on a par with Richelieu Rock, north of the Similan Islands. Indeed, Hin Daeng is easily among the top ten dive sites in South-East Asia. Koh Lanta is an ideal starting point from which to reach these two excellent sites on a day tour.

The journey time from Saladan is about 3 hours, including diving in isolated spots in the sea. Both places are known for having a remarkable diversity of fish and for their strong coral growth. Due to their location, they are frequented by inquisitive deep-sea dwellers.

Fact File

Divers will be best looked after around Saladan in north Koh Lanta. There are several accommodation possibilities here. In some of them, such as the Lanta Island Resort, there is also a diving school.

Diving and living

There is no doubt that Phuket has the broadest range of accommodation on offer. Those in search of a beach or local evening entertainment near their hotel will prefer the west coast. The hinterland is quieter, while Chalong has the advantage of the port used by the diving ships.

Useful Information

Dive Asia

Dive Asia, founded in 1988 on Kata Beach as one of the first dive sites in Phuket, is currently managed by Jürgen Schenker and Benno Brandon. These two diving instructors, with their two big diving boats MV *Dive Asia I* and MV *Dive Asia II*, bring their guests to the best places in the area around Phuket. Their programme includes multi-day and single-day tours. Since 2000, Dive Asia has had a training and technical centre with a special training pool. Nitrox and rebreather diving is on offer, and the centre is open all year round. With its PADI 5 Star CDC centre, Dive Asia offers

Above The liveaboard boat MV *Dive Asia I*

Opposite The training pool at the Dive Asia diving centre.

guests in Kata, Karon and Patong a collection service to and from their hotels. *www.diveasia.com*.

Sea Bees Phuket

The headquarters of Holger Schwab's long-established diving centre, Sea Bees, is in Phuket, in the Chalong area. Located along the small access road to the pier at Chalong Bay, you can reach the harbour from here in a matter of minutes. The diving school offers not only PADI-based programmes but also courses for CMAS or Barracuda certificates. It offers trips to the dive sites to the east and south of Phuket in the day boat MV *Excalibur*. Depending on the season, multi-day trips to this area or to the Similan Islands are undertaken in the MV *Marco Polo*. Sea Bees is one of the few diving centres to have its own resort, which lies only 5 minutes on foot from the centre of Chalong. The first lessons of the beginner diving course also take place in the pool at the centre. *www.sea-bees.com*.

Fact File

Right next to the Sea Bees Diving Centre is the Anchor Inn restaurant, managed by Jackie and Poukie Sengchat. As well as the local cuisine, there are also many European dishes on the menu.

Ao Nang

There is accommodation of various types and variable quality in and around Ao Nang. Among the best hotels in the area, and thus favoured by many holidaymakers, is the Krabi Thai Village Resort. It is in a quiet location hardly more than 5 minutes from the promenade, and it has various types of rooms, from very appealing standard bedrooms up to extremely elegant deluxe options (*www.krabithaivillage.com*).

In Ao Nang there are several multilingual diving centres. Some are located on the promenade. Depending on the weather and the season, longer journeys are usually made by speedboat, while those to locations in the immediate vicinity use the local long-tail boats.

Diving centres on the internet include Coral Diving (*www.coraldiving.com*) and the Poseidon Dive Centre (*www.poseidon-krabi.com*).

Some diving centres in Ao Nang change the trips offered depending on the season. This may mean that some trips to more distant dive sites are cancelled due to a lack of participants.

Fact File

The Sub Aqua Dive Centre is located in the prestigious Hilton Resort Phuket. The hotel is located on the west coast opposite the beach. Nitrox 32 provided free. www.subaquadivecenter.com

Koh Lanta

This island lies about 70 km south of Krabi on the east coast of Phang Nga Bay. It stretches 27 km in a north–south direction. There is a chain of large and small hills throughout most of Koh Lanta, partly covered by tropical rainforest. The beaches for which Koh Lanta is famous are located on the west coast, extending northwards up to the town of Saladan. There are several resorts located here. In addition to the superior Chada Beach Resort (*www.chadabeachresort.com*), an upmarket hotel that has Koh Lanta's biggest swimming pool, the most highly recommended area is the reasonably priced Lanta Island Resort, which is also open all year round (*www.lantaislandresort.com*). This facility, with its pretty garden bungalows, lies directly opposite the sea. The restaurant and bar offer a view of the sunset every evening.

Previous double page In the pool (**above left**) and on board the *Excalibur*, the dive ship of Sea Bees Phuket (**below left**). The exclusive Krabi Thai Village (**below right**).

This page The Ko Lanta Diving Center.

A recommended hotel is the Lanta Island Resort.

Right next to the hotel restaurant on the beach is a branch of Christian Miets' Ko Lanta Diving Center. The headquarters of the diving school is in Saladan, from where the diving boat departs. Christian Mietz, an author with an excellent knowledge of Thailand, provides both day trips and two-day trips with his ships, offering tours to places such as Hin Daeng and Hin Muang (*www.kolantadivingcenter.com*).

One of the Ko Lanta Diving Center's liveaboard boats.

At a Glance

★ *about 4 km south-west of Ao Nang*
⚓ *30-minute journey by long-tail boat*
⊗ *5–15 m*
⊙ *10–25 m*
↻ *no current to moderate currents possible*
⊛ *half-day tour, also very well suited to snorkellers*
▣ *suitable for beginners*

Koh Si

Koh Si is a group of three rocks that are connected below the surface of the sea. At one point, between two of the rocks, you can dive from one side of the group to the other with no problem. Thus, divers whose air consumption is not all that high can perform a 'round trip' through the area.

The advantage of the island dive sites is that even in a high wind the relatively small long-tail boats can easily anchor in shelter on the leeward side. Divers can then decide whether to stay on this side of the reef or whether – as long as the currents are weak or non-existent – they want to dive to the other side of the island.

A ring of hard corals has grown around the Koh Si formation; it is particularly visible on the west side. Antler and horn corals extend over reasonably large areas, and small coral fish find refuge among their branches. However, this is also the hunting ground of eels, and the black-and-white ringed highly poisonous banded sea krait ('sea cobra').

The Koh Si diving area is a place for beginners; it may pose difficulties, but the chances are it won't, and usually even moderate currents do not cause much trouble. The diving depth at the edge of the corals (bordering the sand) is barely 15 m, and this too means that no great demands will be placed on the diver.

Although generally classified as a beginner's area, Koh Si is known for having a wide range of interesting sea life. In the southern stretches, there are so-called barrel or cup corals, while

Right When encountering sea snakes, such as this venomous banded sea krait, take care!

Opposite The eye of a pufferfish (**above**). Blue-spotted stingrays resemble blue-spotted ribbontail rays (**below**).

Following double page Koh Si consists of three rock towers which form a massif beneath the surface of the water.

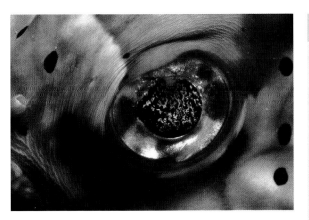

whip corals grow between sponges. Small stingrays are also part of the fauna here, as are several species of prawn, a variety of nudibranchs and seahorses.

Those who have enough leisure time available and who can stay in a single place for a longer period of time will get to see small barracuda passing through here in shoals. You may also encounter a variety of snappers and coral fish. Sometimes, with a bit of luck, you will even get to see leopard sharks on the sandy border.

Safety Tips

The banded sea krait is a snake whose deadly venom is far stronger than that of any snake on land. However, their fangs are relatively far back in the mouth and they cannot tear with their jaws, as other snakes can. But they can easily bite the skin between the thumb and the index finger or an earlobe. This can happen if you get in the way of a snake that is moving quickly back to the sea bed after surfacing. Because there is no readily available antidote, any bite from this snake is likely to be extremely dangerous.

Koh Talu

At a Glance

★ about 4 km
south-west of Ao
Nang
⏳ 30-minute
journey by long-tail
boat
⊗ 5–15 m
👁 10–25 m
↻ moderate to no
currents
🐠 a good place for
seahorses
▣ suitable for
beginners

The island of Koh Talu is known for its grottos and caves. There is a large passage from one side of the island to the other that is only a few metres long, and wide enough that even beginners can dive through it without difficulty. There is also a second tunnel, which should also pose no problem for inexperienced divers. Many hard corals have grown on the west side of Koh Talu. The extensive fields of staghorn corals are also noteworthy.

In the large passage, the ground is barely 10 m deep. Seahorses live in the entrance area on the west side and in the passage itself. They prefer to hang around the branches of the sea fans. At times, you can find more than half a dozen of these animals at Koh Talu.

This dive site is a straightforward, simple beginner's area. The coral growth only stretches away from the island in the south, and divers should take careful note of their route there.

Koh Talu is a big, solitary rock.

Opposite Seahorses like hanging around the sea fans.

Below To the south, the coral field stretches away from the island.

At a Glance

Koh Ha

★ *about 5 km
south-west of Ao
Nang*
⛵ *35-minute
journey by long-tail
boat*
☼ *5–20 m*
👁 *5–25 m*
↩ *no current to
moderately strong
currents*
🐠 *many different
types of hard coral*
▨ *suitable for
beginners*

Koh Ha lies a few hundred metres west of Koh Si, and is the furthest of the islands from Ao Nang. The island looks like just another
rock, typical of the islands of Ao Nang. The island group of the
same name south-west of Koh Lanta has no connection with the
Koh Ha near Ao Nang.

The visibility in the waters around Koh Ha is sometimes limited, but this also applies to most of the other dive sites in the
region. One thing that stands out here is the diversity of the hard
corals, of which dozens of different species have been identified
in Koh Ha. There are also sea fans, but they are clearly outnum-
bered by the hard corals. Particularly impressive are a number of
big funnel corals that resemble cups – some of them are down-
right gigantic. Coral fish scurry around, although they are not
strikingly numerous. Nudibranchs, on the other hand, are plentiful and easy to spot.

Fact File

Beginner divers should take particular care to ensure good buoyancy when they hover above staghorn corals. Their very fragile structure will not bear any weight, but will break off with the slightest clumsy touch. In these situations it is also important to secure dangling instruments (such as a pressure gauge on the end of a tube) closely to your body. Otherwise, as you swim just above the corals, they can get caught in the branches and even break them.

Above With a bit of patience, you will also get a chance to see lively and colourful angelfish.

Below One of the best-known types of coral is the spreading table coral.

Opposite The only thing that Koh Ha (Ao Nang) has in common with the Koh Ha island group (Koh Lanta) is its name.

Koh Doc Mai

★ *about 15 km east of Phuket*
🚤 *whole-day tours from Chalong Bay/ Phuket*
⊗ *5–30 m*
👁 *5–25 m*
↻ *weak to moderate currents*
🐟 *beautifully covered steep walls, fantastic for close-up photography*
🔲 *for experienced divers*

The 'Flower Island' – its Thai name – can be reached by boat in about an hour from the diving centres of Chalong Bay. Because of this, as well as the fact that a steep wall dive is possible under almost any weather conditions or in any wind, the area is a very popular dive site.

To the east of the island, and especially to the north, the rock falls away steeply to a depth of 30 m. On the west side, it descends somewhat more gradually. Here, more hard corals grow on the sea bed at a depth of about 15 m. However, many divers prefer the east side. This may also be because of the pair of caves. The larger of the two, in the southern part of the east wall, has its entrance at a depth of 18 m. The smaller, almost exactly at the halfway point of the east wall, has its entrance at a depth of about 22 m. Entering the caves is not advised. The island consists of karst, and cave diving in such an environment should only be undertaken by experienced cave divers.

Hard to spot – a frogfish.

The visibility at Koh Doc Mai can vary between 5 and 25 metres.

In places the wall is thickly covered with corals and sponges. In some rock niches, protected against the current, there are ghost pipefish, sometimes perpendicular and sometimes parallel to the coral stems. Discovering one is mostly a matter of patience, because they are often coloured exactly like the coral branches in their surroundings.

Various kinds of nudibranch are a much more common sight. It is also worth looking for dancing shrimps in shady areas.

However, it can be difficult for underwater photographers to spot them. This kind of shrimp likes to jump short distances – hence 'dancing'. Some overhangs are home to sweepers, which live in large shoals. When touched by a spotlight, they bunch up so tightly that they could almost be a wall of small fish.

Last but not least, Koh Doc Mai is a good site for spotting the large seahorses known as tiger tail seahorses. However, being yellow and black in colour – hence the name – they are usually well camouflaged amongst the sponges and corals.

Koh Doc Mai is one of the best dive sites in the region for close-up photography. You should take your time and not be too quick as you dive along the wall, so that you don't miss any of the small-scale beauty.

Opposite There are steep walls almost all the way round the island.

Below Glassy sweepers form dense shoals.

Anemone Reef

Anemone Reef is justifiably considered to be one of the best dive sites in Thailand. It is located about 90 minutes by boat from Chalong harbour, near to Shark Point and the wreck of the ferry *King Cruiser*. The reef's Thai name is Hin Jom, meaning 'submerged rock', which is appropriate. The core of the reef is a karst rock, which starts at a depth of about 30 m and rises to a depth of about 4 m, where it forms a plateau.

At a Glance

★ *about 26 km east of Phuket*
⛴ *whole-day tours from Phuket, Ao Nang, Phi Phi and Koh Lanta*
⊗ *5–30 m*
👁 *5–30 m*
↻ *weak to strong currents*
🐟 *an abundance of fish*
▣ *for experienced divers*

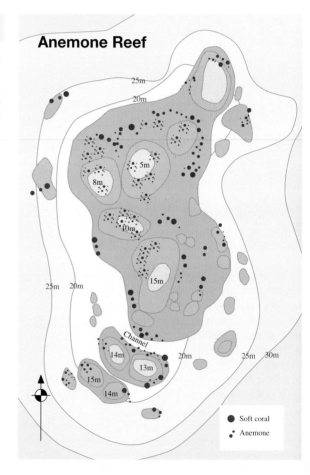

An anemonefish at
Anemone Reef.

The English name Anemone Reef is also apposite, for anemones grow in many places and live in symbiosis with clownfish, also known as anemonefish. The dive site is famous for its immense wealth of fish. Shoals of snappers large and small can be found here, as well as fusiliers and fast swimmers such as barracuda and occasionally the even larger tuna.

Shark Point – only 300 m away – is an even better dive site, at least as far as coral growth is concerned. Nevertheless, in the glow of divers' torches, Anemone Reef with its colourful sponges and soft corals has a lively ambience.

At the foot of the cliff it is not uncommon to find leopard sharks lying in the sand. You may even encounter a whale shark here. The eastern parts of the rock in particular are populated by sweeping

Fact File

*At Anemone Reef,
it is always worth
keeping a lookout
for small sea
creatures in narrow
gaps in the rock
and between coral
branches.*

Previous double page The colourful splendour is only fully appreciated in the torchlight.

Above A banded coral shrimp in a barrel sponge.

Opposite Shark Point is marked by a small lit beacon.

sea fans. However, large barrel sponges prefer the deeper areas. It is always worth looking in their openings: sometimes, cleaner shrimps wait for their customers there.

The best dive run at Anemone Reef begins with a descent to the greatest planned depth. From there, depending on the current around the rocks, you can gradually ascend, circling your way round the rock or zigzagging to the top on the sheltered side.

Much is possible at Anemone Reef, from encounters with whale sharks to observing seahorses, sweepers and other marine attractions.

Shark Point

This spot is named after the frequent encounters with leopard sharks, as well as the other shark species that occur near here. However, it is also very popular among divers because of its exceptional coral growth. Shark Point is only about 300 m from Anemone Reef and the *King Cruiser* wreck, resulting in a travel time of about 90 minutes from Chalong. In contrast to its neighbouring dive sites, Shark Point projects above the water and is marked by a small beacon.

Hin Mu Sang, as Shark Point is called in the native tongue, has been a national park since 1992. It is composed of two rock formations that are almost completely overgrown with corals. The beacon, visible from afar, is located on the northernmost of the two rock complexes. They are located about 15–20 m apart on a north–south axis, separated by a sandy stretch that is approximately 18 m deep. Aside from this channel, the sea bed around the two rocks reaches a depth of about 25 m; further away it can

At a Glance

★ *26 km east of Phuket*

⛴ *whole day tours from Phuket, Ao Nang, Phi Phi and Koh Lanta*

⊗ *3–25 m*

👁 *5–25 m*

↻ *weak to strong current*

🐟 *plentiful coral growth, leopard shark sightings common*

▣ *during weak currents, suitable for beginners; at other times, for more experienced divers*

Shark Point lies near
Anemone Reef.

descend to 30 m or more. Most dive runs begin with a descent at
one of the two rocks and end with an ascent at the other.

Unless the diving guides have set fixed rules, it may be useful
to complete a dive at only one of the two rocks. They are both
big enough, and many fish and small animals live in the coral
landscapes nearby – there is so much to be seen that it is worth
spending a longer period of time there. There are good chances
of sighting shrimps, nudibranchs, seahorses and sweepers.
Naturally, open-water species such as barracuda and batfish can
also be seen around this dive site, as can groupers, scorpionfish,
lionfish and moray eels. Fish are particularly worth watching
at the cleaning stations: flight reactions are far rarer here than
elsewhere.

With a bit of luck, it won't be just leopard sharks that you see around the two rock formations. These sharks are most likely to be found on the adjacent sandy bottom; you may also find the far rarer but no less interesting grey bamboo shark, which also likes

Eye and breathing hole of a grey bamboo shark.

Safety Tips

Divers should not block the escape routes of leopard or other sharks. In such situations, even harmless sharks can become aggressive and attack divers. Their bite is not particularly dangerous, but in many cases nurse sharks and leopard sharks will bite and not let go. There is one known case of a young leopard shark biting into the harness of the jacket of a diver. The belt of the dive jacket had to be cut underwater, because the shark would not loosen its grip. If this happened with an adult shark, the diver's life would be in danger.

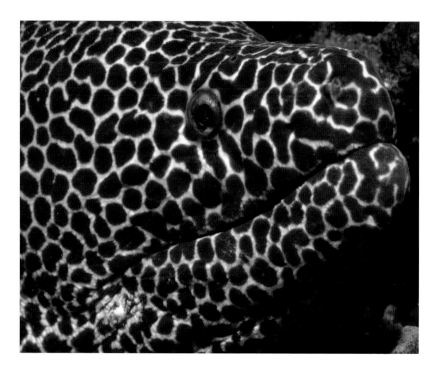

This page Moray eels are not particularly aggressive.

Opposite The *King Cruiser* ferry sank on 4 May 1997, after it ran aground on a rocky reef. *Photo: Sea Bees, Phuket*

lying on the sea bed. This is a harmless species, which typically hides in small caves or under low overhangs. They are normally smaller than leopard sharks and usually uniformly grey, but can also be brownish. They can often be found in the shadows of caves, albeit only with the aid of a torch.

If there is a current, divers should stick to the route between the rocks, just above the sea bed. Under these circumstances, beginners in particular should stay close to the reef, for without a reference point – as in the case of reduced visibility – you can quickly and easily get carried away.

Wreck of the *King Cruiser*

With a length of 85 m and a width of 25 m, the former passenger-car ferry *King Cruiser* is a medium-sized wreck. This ship, which travelled regularly between Phuket and Phi Phi, sank on 4 May 1997 when it ran aground on the shallow underwater rock called Hin Jom – better known among divers as Anemone Reef – and sprang a leak. The ferry took on a list and was evacuated, thankfully with no loss of life, but it did not sink immediately, instead floating on its side for some distance just below the surface. Only about 1.5–2 hours after the accident did the *King Cruiser* finally sink to the sea floor, hundreds of metres from Anemone Reef. It was later discovered that the wreck was upright on the sandy bottom. Of the 600 or so people aboard, none were seriously injured.

The *King Cruiser* was built in Kobe, Japan, and had four decks. The highest point of the wreck is what used to be the bridge. Thus most tours start with a rope descent in the low-lying areas at about 12 m deep, and end at the same point.

At a Glance

★ *26 km east of Phuket*

⚓ *whole-day tours of Phuket, Ao Nang, Phi Phi and Koh Lanta*

✕ *12–32 m*

👁 *5–25 m*

↻ *weak current (though it can strengthen)*

➤ *descent and ascent conducted with the aid of a buoy line*

▣ *under good conditions or led by a diving guide; also for beginners with some experience*

Safety Tips

When visiting wrecks such as the King Cruiser *you should always keep an eye on your depth and your air consumption. If the diving route runs around the bow or the stern, then the way back to the up-line can quickly become difficult if there is a counter-current. To be safe, follow the 'thirds rule': plan one-third of your air consumption for your route out; then, when you start your return route, in ideal circumstances you will have two-thirds of your air supply in reserve. This applies regardless of whether you dive in the hold or whether your dive is limited to viewing the wreck from the outside.*

If you plan on diving at the site of the *King Cruiser* and you want to swim through the loading decks, then in advance of your dive you should make sure to obtain information from the diving centres on the current state of the deck. After all, the steel ship has been decaying since 1997. There are many times when it may seem easy to dive through the window openings from one side of the ship to the other – especially since you can see light coming through from the other side. However, there are parts of the deck towards the stern that have already collapsed. So you should allow for the fact that ongoing corrosion

is liable to weaken the structure of the ship enough to increase the risk of collapse.

The wreck offers something interesting for divers of all levels of experience. However, the average visibility is poor. Divers (particularly the less experienced) should therefore ensure that they are capable of safely finding the ascent line again. The remains of the bridge in the upper regions (down to 15 m deep) can also be visited on a dive when there is a weak to moderate current present. If the current runs from bow to stern or vice versa, there are many structures and sites on the deck that offer shelter from the current. On the other hand, if the current is against the side of the ship, then it may be possible to dive on the leeward side, alongside or underneath the rail. The spacious decks at around 20 m deep can be explored, but beginners should only attempt this under optimal conditions. If visibility is less than 10 m, there is a risk of getting lost. Those who want to dive down to the ship's screws on the sea bed must be absolutely sure in advance that air

Opposite The *King Cruiser* is an attractive dive site, even in the upper levels (**above**). There are some points where you can get a good view of the structure (**below**).

Following double page Over the years, the wreck has become a home for many fish.

Below The *King Cruiser* offers plenty of opportunities for photography.

The scorpionfish are always well camouflaged and easily overlooked.

consumption, ascent time and the influence of currents has been taken into account in the dive plan. If conditions are right, you should begin your dive from the mooring buoy before exploring the ship at the top. If visibility is poor and the current conditions are difficult, then a descent to the ship's screws should be undertaken only by experienced divers.

The marine life in and around the wreck is varied. Leopard sharks are sometimes seen on the sea bed, and you may also spot shoals of smaller fish near the lower decks. Groups of yellowstripe snappers and other members of this family live among the upper decks. Large numbers of pufferfish also seem to have made the wreck their home. Sightings of scorpionfish, and occasionally lionfish, are possible, and close up you can see various types of nudibranchs and aeolid nudibranchs. Soft corals have settled in a few places on the upper deck.

Racha Yai

Racha Yai, which lies north of its sister island Racha Noi, is an island which has about five different dive sites on its south-east side. There are two more which lie east and west of the northern tip, as well as another on the west side of the island, in Bungalow Bay. All sites lie directly off the coast. Because of its position, Racha Yai is an ideal diving area, whatever the weather. There is always excellent visibility around the island, and this, combined

At a Glance

★ 22 km south of Phuket

⚓ multi-day and whole-day tours

⊗ 5–35 m

👁 10–30 m

↷ weak to extremely strong currents

✈ island with several sites

▤ suitable for beginners

Many staghorn corals grow on the fringing reef to the south.

Safety Tips

There are several mooring buoys anchored in the many bays off Racha Yai. During dives in the shallower areas, be aware of boat traffic.

Racha Yai is one of the most versatile dive sites in the east. Large barrel sponges grow here.

with depths averaging between 10 m and 30 m, means that it is suitable for all divers, whatever their experience.

Along the east coast, which runs more or less straight in a south–south-east direction as far as the southernmost tip of Racha Yai, there is a long fringing reef. Hard corals, including the staghorn coral, grow here, extending over a large area. There are also blocks of stone corals, which grow along the entire coastline in the sandy areas. They are particularly prevalent in Siam Bay, at the northern end of the island, and are covered in part by other corals. Barely deeper than 15 m, this spot is good for night diving.

While Siam Bay lies west of the northern foothills of the island, Homerun Reef lies to the east. Here too, the branching staghorn corals dominate long stretches of the reef landscape. Most of the sights which divers will find interesting are at a depth of about 20 m, where several granite rocks can be found.

Siam Bay lies at the northern
end of Racha Yai.

The usual species of coral fish live here, including surgeonfish,
parrotfish and butterfly fish. At such an exposed location you may
also encounter inhabitants of the open sea, such as various types
of barracuda, including the small yellowtail barracuda, or its close
relative the obtuse barracuda. Drift dives can also be carried out
around this reef. Normally the current is light enough that such a
dive can be made without any problems. The remains of a wreck
lie at a depth of about 20 m, but a trip there is by no means a must.

Further south along the coast, near Homerun Reef, there are
dive sites located in or around five small bays, each of which has
simply been assigned a number. The diving schools have designated the northernmost as Bay No. 1 and the southernmost as Bay
No. 5. However, the dive sites merge into one another, and some
sections, such as parts of Bays No. 2 and No. 3, also carry the name
Staghorn Reef, named after the staghorn corals that are charac-

Fact File

The area around Bays No. 3 and No. 4 is also referred to by the diving schools as Lucy's Reef, while No. 5 is also known as Huncy's Reef. Here, larger boulders are located near the shore. This area reaches a depth of around 10–20 m. A moderate current can allow a relaxed drift dive. In principle, it does not matter in which direction this current runs along the coast, as long as the diving boat follows the divers. There is, of course, barely any trace of these currents within the bays themselves.

teristic of the reef just below the surface. The reef is populated by many snappers and fusiliers as well as the yellowtail barracuda that can frequently be seen passing through this region. On a smaller scale, you will of course see the usual coral fish as well as many different kinds of nudibranchs and shrimp.

There are large shoals of emperor bream in these coastal areas. You can see dense shoals of lionfish swimming above the corals, and butterfly fish also pass through the reef, mostly moving in pairs.

Racha Noi South Tip

At the southernmost tip of Racha Noi, the island about 10 km south-east of Racha Yai, the rocky headland under the water spreads out and forms a plateau. The dive site is designated by many diving schools as either South Tip or Plateau. At the end of the expanse, three neighbouring rocks rise from the plateau at a depth of about 16 m. The largest stretches up to 9 m, while the others reach depths of 12 and 14 m. For this area, generally speak-

At a Glance

★ about 32 km south of Phuket, 10 km south-south-west of Racha Yai

⚓ multi-day driving cruises, whole-day tours

✖ 10–40 m and more

👁 10–35 m

↻ strong to very strong currents

⤳ diving area with great average depth

☠ experienced divers only

The thorny oyster grows as large as a dessert plate.

Opposite The yellow-stripe barracuda are usually barely 40 cm long (**above**). The fins of a small boxfish move rather like the rotors of a mini-helicopter (**below**).

Mantas come to Racha Noi in January and February.

ing, great depths can be reached relatively quickly as soon as you move away from the three outcrops. Because of this, and the usually strong currents at the South Tip, the area should only be visited by experienced divers.

The small rocky massif with the three peaks is covered with soft corals. They benefit from the wealth of food brought to them by the strong current, filtering out the plankton. As at many such diving sites, the local marine fauna is varied and sometimes dense. In addition to the lower life forms such as corals or sponges, there are also small coral fish to be found on the reef; particularly butterfly fish and anthias.

The wide range of potential prey attracts many kinds of predators. Among these ever-present hunters are the various types of moray eels. During the day they hide in small caves, mostly resting, but generally with their heads showing as they keep a look out. Their gaping mouths are no threatening gesture – all they are doing is gathering the necessary oxygen supply by allowing the water to flow through their gills. Don't be fooled, though. These muscular animals can attack with lightning speed if they feel threatened or harassed. Moray eels only hunt at dusk,

Above Small moray eels are no less curious than their larger counterparts.

Following double page Corals have evolved into many varieties.

but sometimes they can also be seen swimming through the reef during the day.

Representatives of the scorpionfish family (such as common scorpionfish and lionfish) can also be found here. Divers must be particularly aware of the highly poisonous stonefish. This is especially the case if you need to hold onto a piece of rock with no vegetation in a very strong current. Stonefish are so well camouflaged that you will often not notice them at first. Because they rely on their camouflage and their venom, it is possible that they will not move from their location if you move your hand towards them from above; they will simply erect their strong dorsal spines, through whose channels their poison will be injected, as through a syringe. A stonefish's poison can be deadly. If you absolutely must be in an area with a strong current such as is found at South Tip, then, if at all possible, check the location thoroughly in advance and make absolutely sure that it is safe.

This dive site is ideal for encounters with sharks. Leopard sharks, a common sight all over Thailand, can be found resting on the sandy bottom, and sometimes a black-tip reef shark may swim around the southern end of Racha Noi.

Due to the exposed nature of the southern tip, other open-ocean species, such as fast-swimming tuna or the rainbow runner, are regular visitors. Large schools of barracuda are more tied to the area around Racha Noi. They regularly swim along the reef, forming a giant circle. Mackerel behave in a similar way. Mantas and eagle rays visit the reef mainly during the months of January and February.

The best way of diving in this area is to start your descent above the plateau where the three peaks are located. While you are protected by these rocks, you can judge the state of the currents. In addition, the site is a great place for observing the mantas that like to drift around the area in circles.

Opposite The uninhabited island of Phi Phi Lee is a popular destination for divers and tourists alike.

Hard to spot: the stonefish, whose sting can be deadly, even for humans.

Hin Bida

The Phi Phi Group consists of six islands. The main island is Koh Phi Phi Don, where there are several hotels and some dive schools. However, the most famous of the islands is the uninhabited Phi Phi Lee, about 6.5 sq km in size; it was here, on Maya Bay, that the outdoor scenes for the film *The Beach*, starring Leonardo DiCaprio, were shot. Many day tourists from Phuket or Koh Lanta, but also from Phi Phi Don, visit this area. The Phi Phi Island group has been a national park since 1983.

Diving ships take about 3 hours to get from Phuket to the Phi Phi archipelago, while the journey from Koh Lanta or Ao Nang is about 60–90 minutes shorter. Speedboats manage the distance in half the time.

While some dive sites around Phi Phi Don and Phi Phi Lee are visited only by the local bases, others are visited by vessels from the bases on Ao Nang, Koh Lanta and Phuket. One of these places is Hin Bida, which is also known by some diving schools as the Phi Phi Lee Shark Point. This term, however, is likely to cause

At a Glance

★ *about 43 km east of Phuket, 35 km northwest of Koh Lanta, 30 km from Ao Nang*

⚓ *whole-day tours from Phuket, Ao Nang and Koh Lanta, short journey times from Phi Phi Don*

⊗ *3–26 m*

👁 *5–20 m*

↻ *weak to moderate currents*

🦈 *a good place for spotting leopard sharks*

▣ *for beginner divers with some experience*

Hatchetfish love to shelter in shaded areas.

confusion, for the reef has nothing to do with the similarly named dive site near Anemone Reef and the wreck of the *King Cruiser* (see pages 139–144).

Hin Bida is a small rock formation that lies south-east of Phi Phi Lee. At low tide, a part of the tip can be seen on the surface. The layout of Hin Bida can best be described as elongated. Off the northern side, the ocean floor falls away to a depth of about 15 or 16 m, where it borders the sandy bottom. It is barely more than 21 m deep, even when some distance from the cliff. The elongated south side of Hin Bida is also about 16 m from the surface to the sandy sea bed, but the maximum depth in this direction barely exceeds the 18 m mark. Because leopard sharks are most frequently sighted on the northern side, this area is referred to by some diving centres as Shark Point, as previously mentioned.

Different species of hard corals and a somewhat denser growth of soft corals add colour to the rock. Butterfly fish and angelfish provide lively highlights. Many variously coloured feather stars unfold as soon as dawn breaks. With their claw-like feet they cling to rocks, but also to corals. If you take the time to observe them, you'll notice that despite their apparent lack of mobility they can in fact move at some speed. It is worth taking a close look at the details: sometimes, small crabs (only 2 or 3 cm in size) live between the claws of feather stars.

The visibility in the waters around Hin Bida is often only moderate – averaging between 10 and 15 m – but divers are compensated for this by a diverse population of animals. The snappers that visit here are both larger solitary individuals and smaller fish in large schools. Grunt prefer to stay in one place for a longer period of time, and can be seen both individually and in groups. Some fish look for the protection of the table corals, and observe life from beneath them as from under an umbrella.

A dive at Hin Bida may descend within sight of the highest crag or in its shade, down to the foot of the reef. If conditions permit, you should also be able to spot leopard sharks on the north side.

Elegant squat lobsters live between the arms of individual feather stars.

Hin Bida is popular among divers – and leopard sharks.

Many divers have spoken of seeing several of these species here simultaneously. Larger stingrays may also be encountered on the sandy bottom around Hin Bida.

Grunt are common in the Indo-Pacific area.

Koh Bida Nai

At a Glance

The journey to the karst island of Koh Bida Nai from Phuket takes about 3 hours in a large dive boat. From Koh Lanta or Ao Nang, the journey takes about 2 hours, while this journey time is halved when travelling by speedboat.

Almost directly south of the southern tip of Koh Phi Phi Lee, at a distance of approximately 1 km, lies the small rocky island of Koh Bida Nai. It has an almost semicircular coastline to the north, tapering to a point towards the south. Koh Bida Nai and its neighbouring island Koh Bida Nok, which sticks out of the sea only a few hundred metres away, are both easy to distinguish from afar. The slightly smaller Koh Bida Nai is slightly higher, with a steep-sided towering peak. The slightly more southerly Koh Bida Nok, although equally towering, is more regularly shaped at its highest point, and looks slightly dome-shaped from a distance.

Although the two islands are close together, their reef structures differ under the water. The sea bed around Bida Nai is littered with boulders of various sizes, except for a stretch along the north side. Where they overlap each other, small caves have formed in some places. Such an overlap has formed a tunnel-like

★ *about 43 km east of Phuket, 35 km north-west of Koh Lanta, 30 km from Ao Nang*

⛴ *whole-day tours from Phuket, Ao Nang and Koh Lanta, short travel times from Phi Phi Don*

⊗ *5–30 m*

👁 *5–20 m*

↻ *no current to moderate current*

⌁ *neighbouring island to Koh Bida Nok*

▨ *suitable for beginners*

Left More soft corals and fan corals grow around the north side.

Right Cup sponges are often over 1 m tall.

Previous page Bida Nai is slightly smaller than Bida Nok.

passage just to the west of the southern tip of Bida Nai, at a depth of about 12 m; it can even be dived through. Not far from this, at the southernmost point of the reef, is a rock whose peak is at a depth of about 10 m. There is a mooring buoy anchored about midway between these two points.

However, the underwater landscape on the sea bed is not just made up of boulders. Almost the entire southern half of the island is surrounded by a wreath of various hard corals. In addition to staghorn corals, small-polyp hard corals such as *Montipora aequituberculata* – a very slow-growing coral – can also be found on the reef. Table corals, of course, are also found here, but most of them seem to have settled along the east coast, roughly halfway down the reef. Most staghorn corals are located in this area. There are also shoals of glassy sweepers around many caves and overhangs. It is worth being on the lookout for cleaning stations in this area, where even very shy fish will remain for a while (as long as divers do not approach them too quickly).

The north side of Koh Bida Nai is home to soft corals, sea fans and also some large bucket or barrel sponges. In this area, the ground slopes quite steeply. A few metres from the foot of the cliff the sea bed reaches a depth of more than 25 m before descending rapidly to 30 m.

On the east side the sandy bottom, with its large field of staghorn corals, is flatter. Angelfish and butterfly fish swim through the coral formations, and the sandy zone is a preferred resting place for leopard sharks.

On the south-east side of the island, separate from the reef, is a small group of rocks. There are three points where it reaches up to 14–16 m below the surface. The formation is located on sloping ground, and thus the depth gauge will show between 15 and 20 m on the side facing the island. This is also the location of the anchor of another mooring line. On the opposite side of the cliffs, depths of almost 30 m are reachable. The rocks are partially overgrown with soft corals and some sea fans, while at the top there are a few whip corals.

This point, located a short distance away from Koh Bida Nai, is also a good spot for observing the large schools of barracuda that regularly pass through the water near the island. Bigeye treval-

Fact File

If the rock tower in the south-east is to be included in the diving plan, then it is recommended that you begin your dive route there. This is the deepest area of the site; thus you can remain at lower depths on the island itself and finally emerge there.

These soft corals have encrusted a dead branch of a black coral tree.

lies can also be seen in comparable numbers, although not quite as often. Black-tip reef sharks are perennially present at Bida Nai, as well as occasional white-tip reef sharks.

As for the smaller species, there are many nudibranchs, and even ghost pipefish, living in the reef on the island. The best place to find this rare species is between the branches of the soft corals on the north side.

This page Butterfly fish usually move through the reef in pairs.

Opposite Koh Bida Nok, shown here to the left of Bida Nai, offers spectacular underwater landscapes.

Koh Bida Nok

As with the whole Phi Phi island group, Koh Bida Nok can be reached from Phuket in around 3 hours. The journey here from Koh Lanta or Ao Nang (Krabi) takes about 2 hours. The neighbouring island of Koh Bida Nai rises from the sea with vertical cliffs almost all the way round.

The underwater landscape around Koh Bida Nok is similarly spectacular. With the exception of the south side, where there is a small bay, the sea bed descends steeply to its greatest depth a short distance from the foot of the island. The most significant drop-off is located on the north-west corner of the island. Here, the island wall finishes at a depth of about 20 m, and the ground instantly drops again, soon exceeding the 30 m mark. A large part of the wall is thickly overgrown with soft corals. If you dive around the northern tip, with the reef on your left, after a while you will see a small cave at a depth of about 20 m – one which should only be dived through in the company of a guide. As on the north side, the wall here is also covered with colourful soft corals and sea fans.

At a Glance

★ about 43 km east of Phuket, 35 km north-west of Koh Lanta, 30 km from Ao Nang

⛴ whole-day tours from Phuket, Ao Nang and Koh Lanta, short travel times from Phi Phi Don

🌀 5–30 m

👁 5–20 m

🔄 none to moderate current

🐠 the most beautiful dive spot of the Phi Phi group of islands

▣ suitable for beginners

When exploring the entrance to the cave in the northern part of the west side, you must ensure that there are no whirling floating particles. Only divers with experience of cave diving should proceed further into the cave, as is always the case with such conditions.

Along the stretch of coastline running from the north to the east, many small rocks lie underwater. Here, the sea bed descends less dramatically. The 25 m contour runs in a curved arc, some distance from the east coast of Bida Nok, while rock debris and coral rocks lie just below the wall. Solitary big snappers frequent these spots. Sometimes, they hide under table corals and jump out in front of divers right at the last moment. Leopard sharks are also frequently seen resting in the sand, and often several can be seen during a diving run. Stingrays can also be seen from time to time.

South-east of the island, an underwater tongue of rock extends a short way from Bida Nok. As it has an average depth of only 15m, it is an ideal place to spend a longer period of time. To the sides, the ground slopes more gently away from the island. Schools of smaller fish seem to enjoy hanging around the colourfully overgrown rocks.

There is a good chance of sighting a turtle in this area. Turtles eat green bubble coral, among other things. Once they have dis-

covered a source of food, they rarely allow themselves to be distracted. Divers can get very close to the animals – approach them
slowly and make no sudden movements.

To the west of the rock tongue, the small bay of Koh Bida Nok
lies above the surface. Even underwater, the course of the sea
bed largely follows the coastline. From the upper reaches, at a
depth of 5–6 m, it extends into the outlet of the bay, where the
cliffs and the hard corals end, at a depth of around 15–20 m. A
short distance along, in the mouth of the bay, you will encounter another colourfully overgrown rock, which rises up to 12 m.
It is worth keeping your eyes open for ghost pipefish between

Opposite A lionfish lies in
wait for the small fish which
romp between staghorn
corals.

Below Large snappers
are solitary – and have a
powerful bite.

Following double page
If you approach feeding
turtles carefully, they rarely
show fear.

Fact File

When there is a current, a drift dive along the west side of Koh Bida Nok is recommended. However, if the opportunity arises and you have sufficient air available, a visit to the tongue of rock in the south-east is a must.

the coral branches. As in other places, this reef also has a huge abundance of fish.

If you dive clockwise further along the island from here, you will reach the southernmost point of the reef. Here there is a small rocky pinnacle, whose highest point is only 5 m below the surface. When following the sea bed at 20 m, you encounter further coral formations.

As with its sister island Koh Bida Nai, there is a tunnel near the south-west tip of Koh Bida Nok, which can be dived through. On the outside, the opening is about 16 m deep, while the passage on the other side ends at about 12 m.

Koh Ha 1

To the west of Koh Lanta, about 1 hour away by large dive boat, lies a small archipelago composed of five small rock islands. The whole group lies on a north–south axis and is called Koh Ha. In the local dialect, *ha* is the word for five. The name does not correspond entirely with the facts: if you look closely you see a rock that could count as the group's sixth island. As with the Similans – and as is often the case in Thailand – these uninhabited islands do not just have Thai names, but are also identified by sequential numbers. In contrast to the sequence in the Similans, here it is Island No. 1 that is the northernmost of the small archipelago. Its sides, almost equal in length, lie on an east–west axis. At the western end, the island is roughly crescent-shaped, with a small cape located on the eastern tip.

At a Glance

★ *about 25 km west of Koh Lanta, 85 km south-east of Phuket*

⛴ *whole-day tours from Koh Lanta, Ao Nang and Phi Phi or on multi-day trips*

⊗ *5–30 m*

👁 *10–30 m*

↻ *light to moderate currents*

➹ *island reef with steep sides and diverse marine life; the 'Chimney' cave*

▣ *suitable for beginners*

Opposite There are no fewer than 26 species of barracuda worldwide.

This page The Koh Ha island group can be seen from Koh Lanta, on the western horizon.

In the area around Koh Ha Neua (Island No. 1's real name), the sea bed drops off sharply in all locations. On the north side, the ground reaches a depth of 20 m a relatively short distance from the island, and a little after that the depth gauge will read 25 m. Many soft corals grow along the wall, creating a splash of colour. Exactly halfway along the north coast lie three bigger rocks at a depth of 25 m, which are partially covered with corals, including sea fans. Their highest points are 12 and 18 m. The sandy area which runs to the left and right of them is clearly a popular meeting place for leopard sharks.

The fragile fire corals have powerful burning stings.

When diving eastwards along the north coast (i.e. the 'right shoulder' reef), you will reach a cave at a depth of about 12 m. Here, a colony of sand eels has become established on the sea bed. As soon as divers approach them, these animals, barely as thick as a finger, dive back into their holes. If you feel like waiting, they will eventually rise back out of their holes like sprouting flowers – but keep your air consumption and decompression time in mind.

To the north of the eastern tip lies another, significantly larger rock. Its tip reaches up to a depth of about 5 m, while its sides disappear into the ground at a depth of 25 m. Divers have always told stories of the ghost pipefish that live around this rock. Many of these species stay close to a single spot for a long time.

Some sea fans definitely live up to their name in every respect.

Above Snappers of various kinds often gather in small groups, and sometimes in large shoals.

Opposite Batfish often seek the company of divers (**above**). Turtles live in depths of up to about 20 m (**below**).

From the eastern tip up to about halfway along the south side of the island, another field of hard corals has formed from the shallow-water zone to about 15 m, sometimes descending to almost 20 m. At its deepest, the last ring is mostly made up of staghorn corals.

Exactly halfway along the south side, the cliffs, which can reach depths of up to 20 m, are lined with tunnels that can be dived through. In places the rocks are vividly coloured. To the south-west there is another overhang/tunnel combination.

The whole Koh Ha island group consists of karst and is riddled with holes, crevices and caves. No. 5 has a few, but perhaps the most spectacular underwater cave is on its south side. The so-called 'Chimney' is a shaft that rises steeply upwards; its entry point lies at a depth of 16 m, and its exit point at 6 m.

Safety Tips

When diving through tunnels, perfect buoyancy control is essential.

At a Glance

★ *about 25 km west of Koh Lanta, 85 km south-east of Phuket*
🛥️ *whole-day tours from Koh Lanta, Ao Nang and Phi Phi or during multi-day trips*
⊗ *5–25 m*
👁️ *10–30 m*
↪ *mostly only moderate currents*
🐠 *excellent panoramic area with ghost pipefish, harlequin shrimp and nudibranchs among others, often good visibility*
🎴 *suitable for beginners*

Koh Ha Lagoon (Islands 2 and 4)

There are multiple red mooring buoys to be seen between and next to Koh Ha Islands 2, 3 and 4. The islands lie about 100 m from each other, and the buoys in the centre of the island triangle indicate a dive site which, while not spectacular, is still very beautiful. You will not find steep cliffs here. Instead you will find a tremendous variety of fauna. There are also larger marine creatures, such as lobsters, moray eels and octopus, which are fond of hiding

The Koh Ha Group is a fantastically varied dive site.

The dive site referred to as a lagoon is located between Islands 2, 3 and 4.

in small crevices and caves during the day. Sea creatures find an abundance of such hiding places in the soft karst rock of Islands No. 2 and No. 4.

East of these lie the deeper parts of the dive site. When you dive between the rock towers, you pass a small field of soft corals on the sandy bottom at depths of between 10 and 20 m. After that, your destination should be one of the two outer coasts of the islands. On Island No. 4, to the south, down to a depth of about 25 m, there are about half a dozen larger rocks and several smaller ones. Schools of snapper are almost omnipresent. At the southernmost tip of No. 4 there is a beautiful overhang at a depth of about 18 m. A bit further on and closer to the surface, in the western foothills of the island, there is a tunnel that can be dived through.

Many small coral blocks have formed on the north-west coast of No. 2, and you will often find larger eels here. But an even greater attraction is the south-eastern side of Koh Ha No. 2. Whole schools of fish can be found here, including small, bright orange anthias. Just like its counterpart in the south, the eastern side of the northern rocky cliff is, for the most part, covered with various types of colourful corals and sponges. The soft and fan corals do not reach record-breaking proportions here, but they do add a lot of colour to the reef.

The lagoon itself lies west of Island No. 2 and north-west of Island No. 4. There is usually only a weak current here, which generally runs from north to south or vice versa – and if it is too strong, Islands No. 2 and No. 4 always offer a sheltered side to allow for easier diving. The further in the direction of Island No. 3 you dive, the shallower the dive site gets. The depth between the rock towers of No. 2 and No. 4 is still around 10 m, but your depth gauge will not show more than 5 m as soon as you are to the west of these islands.

Right A moray eel among the hard coral rocks to the west of Island No. 2.

Opposite The water in the lagoon is less than 10 m deep (**above**). Like all groupers, the jewel grouper defends a fixed territory (**below**).

Hin Muang

While the neighbouring reef of Hin Daeng is visible above the water, there is not much of Hin Muang to be seen above the surface. However, under the water there is a hidden reef with spectacular encircling cliffs. It is said to be the deepest in the Kingdom of Thailand. The reef is shaped rather like a baguette, lying on an east–west axis. It is about 200 m long and an average of 20 m wide.

Hin Muang has probably the deepest cliff in Thailand.

The blackspotted moray is a beautiful representative of this awe-inspiring family.

Aside from the well-known large species, there are also smaller species of barracuda, such as these obtuse barracuda.

Fact File

Its prominent location in the sea makes this reef a preferred port of call for many pelagic species. Together with Hin Daeng, it is one of the best places in southern Thailand to see whale sharks and mantas. From time to time, even grey reef sharks visit this area. Leopard sharks are also regular inhabitants of a reef of this type.

The reef has five peaks along its length. One is located at each end, and the other three rise up like a mountain range towards the centre. The highest point at the western tip is at a depth of 8 m and is well suited for diving. There are many sea anemones here. One of the two mooring buoys is also anchored nearby, at around 15 m. A channel at a depth of 20 m separates this first peak from the next. The central underwater hills have minimum depths of 12, 14 and 16 m. Beyond the last of these lies another channel, separating it from the easternmost peak. This eastern peak rises up to around 16 m. The second mooring buoy is located here.

Above Grey reef sharks are occasionally seen at Hin Muang.

Below Groupers are often seen in the upper zones of the reef.

Bigeye trevally form large circles just like barracuda.

The steep cliffs around the reef are thickly covered with soft corals, sea fans and black corals. In addition to this coral growth, the fauna of Hin Muang is remarkably diverse. As well as the open-water fish, such as barracuda, bigeye and other species of mackerel, various sharks and large rays, groupers, moray eels and reef fish also live here. At a smaller scale, you will find almost everything that the sea around Thailand has to offer, from harlequin shrimps to ghost pipefish and a wide variety of nudibranchs.

At a Glance

★ *about 50 km south of Koh Lanta, 100 km south-east of Phuket, 90 km south-south-east of Phi Phi Island*

⛴ *whole-day tours from Koh Lanta and Phi Phi, or during multi-day cruises*

✖ *5–45 m*

👁 *5–30 m*

↺ *moderate to strong currents*

➤ *cliff dives, thick coral growth, whale sharks and mantas*

▣ *for intermediate divers*

Hin Daeng

Hin Daeng – which means 'red rock' in Thai – is without doubt one of the best diving areas in the whole of South-East Asia. The reef is often compared to Richelieu Rock, north of the Similan Islands – a kind of underwater mountain with three peaks. They are comparable for two reasons. First, neither is an island, but the three peaks of Hin Daeng project above the water just like Richelieu Rock. Second, both dive sites are indisputably among the best in Thailand for encounters with whale sharks and mantas.

Hin Daeng is about 100 km from the island of Phuket and about 90 km from Koh Phi Phi, so the diving centres based in those locations only visit this area as part of multi-day trips. On the other hand, normal diving vessels (not speedboats) can reach the area from Koh Lanta in about 3 hours.

The Thai name 'red rock' (which was probably given to it by fishermen) may or may not refer to the red corals that grow on Hin Daeng. Whatever the origin of the name, the rock massif is indeed covered in various species of coral – even overgrown in some places. The area is inhabited by an abundance of invertebrates and associated distinct groups of fauna, both territorial reef dwellers and open-water fish.

Hin Daeng

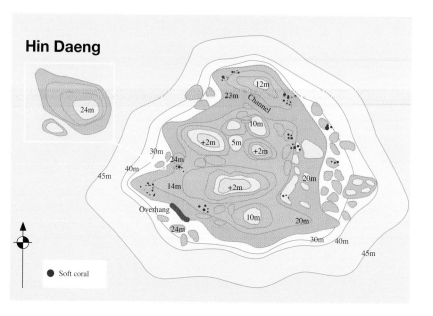

The most impressive part of the dive site is a steep cliff which runs along the south side of the Hin Daeng formation. The cliff ends at about 30 m, then the sandy sea bed descends to 40 m or more. Halfway along the wall, there is a small overhang at a depth of about 16 m.

About 100 m off the west side of Hin Daeng is a large rock. This should not be confused with the neighbouring reef of Hin Muang, which lies about 300 m east of Hin Daeng. The ground around this separate large rock at Hin Daeng is about 50 m deep. With its roughly oval shape, the highest point reaches up to about 25 m. However, the main rocky massif of Hin Daeng is so rich in corals, fish and other animals that it is simply not worth the trip to the rock. There is nothing there that is not also seen at Hin Daeng.

Opposite Hin Daeng is one of the best dive sites in the whole of South-East Asia.

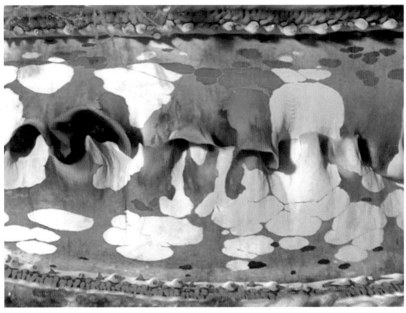

Thorny oyster.

One of the most beautiful places around Hin Daeng is the steep wall to the south. North of this underwater mountain, a canyon runs from east to west, at a depth of about 23 m. Both of Hin Daeng's mooring buoys lie close to these two locations.

Schools of fish, like these snappers, head through the reef in dense shoals.

Around the large rock, with a bit of luck you will see ghost pipefish or harlequin shrimps. Barracuda, fusiliers and groups of batfish roam near or over the rocks. Hin Daeng is also well known for the schools of mackerel that reside here. Snappers of various sorts are also regular visitors.

Leopard sharks are a fairly common sight on the sandy bottom around the rock walls. During the mating season of April and May, a male and a female will often swim in single file through the reef, a prelude to mating. While thus occupied, the harmless leopard sharks will not be distracted by anything and will even swim close by passing divers.

Hin Daeng has the steepest drop-off point of any of Thailand's dive sites. If you have enough time to visit this dive site you should seize the opportunity. You can easily visit on a day trip from Koh Lanta – the journey time is about 3 hours each way – but some dive centres in Phuket also offer tours to Hin Daeng, over a period of 2 days, or during a week-long diving safari.

Above Hin Daeng is a good place for sighting mantas.

Following double page
The jewel grouper is a lively splash of colour in the reef.

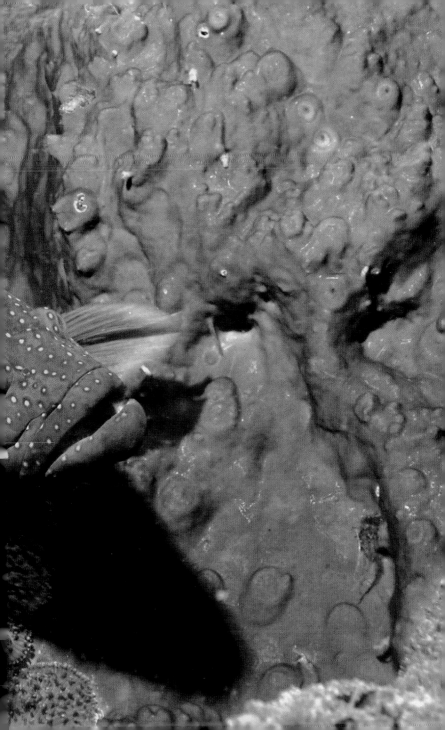

Exotic Charms on Land

Away from Diving

Many divers choose their holiday destination based solely on the attractiveness of the dive sites. For others, their priorities are exactly the opposite: it's all down to the environment, and if you can dive there as well, so much the better. With this in mind, the following section looks at the holiday resorts rather than the diving centres. These, too, have developed markedly in recent times.

Khao Lak

This coastal resort to the north of the island of Phuket is about an hour's drive from Phuket airport, depending on traffic. It is particularly suitable for holidaymakers who want to lie on a beautiful beach. There are more than enough of these, for Khao Lak and the surrounding area has 15 km of the finest sandy beaches.

Hotels here are pleasantly simple. Small or medium-sized resorts are common, and there are no anonymous hotel fortresses. On the other hand, there are also some classy villas, where the cost of staying will vary depending on the number of rooms. As exemplified by Le Meridien, north of Khao Lak, they are usually very well designed. However, those looking for nightlife will not find it in or around Khao Lak.

Phuket

On the west coast, tourism flourishes in its most vibrant form. In Patong Beach you will find all manner of bars, restaurants and discos – this is the right place for holidaymakers who wish to turn night into day. Quieter hotels can be found in Kata and Karon. Each of these three locations has its own beach, but these are of course busier than those near Khao Lak. Divers who want to stay on Phuket but who would prefer to be away from the crowd, while still in a resort, should contact the diving centres listed in the *useful information* section (page 29). They will be able to provide advice on current accommodation.

Ao Nang

This holiday resort in Krabi is a cross between Khao Lak and Phuket. The beach front is very popular throughout the day, even if the beach is not what you'd call a bathing beach. The bathing

Patong Beach is known for its many parasols.

beaches lie to the south of the centre. There is a promenade of souvenir shops here, along with many restaurants, supermarkets and some bars. Nightlife here is also more varied than in Khao Lak, but it does not reach the heights of Patong.

All in all, Ao Nang is unusual, not least because of the salesmen in the souvenir shops, who seem to speak more languages than all of the tourists who have ever visited.

Koh Lanta

This is the place for divers who want to enjoy peace and quiet out of the water – albeit within limits, for even on Koh Lanta you will find one or two beach bars where no drink will be served without appropriate music playing. However, this is as lively as it gets. Saladan is a town where most streets are shuttered as soon as dusk sets in. You will have to search for a disco – you will not just stumble across one as you would in other resorts.

Idyllic beaches can be found in many places away from the resort centres.

Sex, nudists and toplessness

Although many Europeans believe that Thailand is quite relaxed when it comes to sex and erotica, this is not the case. As in many other holiday destinations, this applies only at the relevant establishments.

Tan-line-free sunbathing and swimming is actually strictly forbidden in Thailand. Going topless is also officially not allowed. However, it is now commonly tolerated in many tourist centres, such as on the large beaches of Phuket and Khao Lak and in other resorts. But it is wise for a woman to avoid drawing attention to herself in any case, and to choose almost line-free sunbathing or bathe in a more secluded spot.

Excursions

In addition to the beauty of its underwater world, Thailand is a tourist destination that has many interesting sights to offer on land. Everywhere that is recognized as a holiday destination for divers also has several worthwhile attractions, ranging from off-shore islands and nature reserves to fairytale temples.

Khao Lak

This coastal village with its endlessly long sandy beach lies at the foot of the mountain from which it takes its name. The rainforest in the upper half of Khao Lak is a nature park that you can hike to on foot. Less strenuous is an elephant trek organized by Holiday Service Khao Lak (holiday-service-khaolak.com/en). You will get to ride on the back of an elephant through the tropical rainforest for an hour or more, depending on the tour. Or you can have a go at other activities, such as bamboo rafting on a small river (a local guide steers the raft). In the silence, broken only by the sounds of the forest, with a bit of luck you will even see tree snakes crawling through the branches.

The famous sandy beach of Khao Lak.

An elephant trekking tour through the rainforest is one of the attractions of a holiday in Thailand.

A visit to the Khao Sok National Park and its reservoir, north of Khao Lak, is a popular day trip. If you feel like spending a night or more on the water, there is even accommodation available in a floating village. This unique resort is located on the shore, and walks with a local guide are possible at almost any time.

Mid-way between these two destinations in terms of both time and distance is the island of Koh Kho Khao. For a few baht, you can make the crossing by ferry. Cars and mopeds can be rented in Khao Lak. On the island, you can enjoy a protracted stop in the snack bar of the Amandara Island Resort, located on a long and secluded stretch of beach – ideal for relaxing.

Phuket

Many holidaymakers enjoy the nightlife of Patong. During the day, however, many will visit the beach at Kata with its golden snake sculpture before returning to the peace and quiet of holiday homes.

A popular and culturally significant destination near Chalong is the Wat Chalong (*wat* means temple). This is the largest temple on the island of Phuket, and it is very impressive. The giant Buddha statue on the mountain in the middle of the island will be completed as soon as the monks on the island have collected enough donations. It will then be the largest in Thailand.

Phuket is the traditional tourist centre of Thailand.

It is often said that there are no longer any isolated beaches in Phuket, but this is not the case. It is just that they are not often mentioned. The staff at the diving centres know best, from personal experience – and they can offer the best advice. Elephant trekking is also available on Phuket.

Ao Nang

Some of the small uninhabited islands around the holiday resort of Ao Nang, which also serve as local dive sites for the island's diving centres, can be visited as destinations on day trips. Here, you are as likely to find snorkelling equipment as sun cream.

In the hinterland lies the large Khao Phanom Bencha National Park with its waterfalls. Not far away is the Tiger Cave. You head up about 1000 steps to the summit above the cave. During the ascent to the big Buddha statue, which takes a good 45 minutes, you will pass wild monkeys and will eventually be rewarded with a fantastic view.

The demanding climb to the Buddha statue above the Tiger Cave is rewarded with a fantastic view.

Fact File

Before the days of tourism, in rural areas the owners of rubber plantations were among the richest people. If a family owned land in the coastal region the tradition was that the sons inherited the land in the hinterland with the plantations, while the daughters inherited the areas that were not as desirable, such as the less fertile beaches. Rubber plantations still earn money – but the daughters of yesteryear are these days usually more affluent than their brothers.

Koh Lanta

The National Park of Koh Lanta is located right in the south of the island. On the shore, on a cliff next to the beach, stands a lighthouse – the symbol of the island and a popular photo opportunity. Although Saladan in the north has become an important holiday resort, the capital of Koh Lanta is located in the centre of the island. Both the small shops on the narrow main street and the market are worth a detour. The old island temple lies nearby.

If you want to get to know the island for more than its diving potential, you should plan to spend at least one full day there.

The lighthouse – an emblem of Koh Lanta.

The Muslim fishing village of Koh Panyi.

Fact File

Thai cuisine is world-famous. Inexpensive local food can be found everywhere, whether in a simple restaurant with main dishes starting from about £1/$1.50 – soft drinks can be bought for 50p/80c and beer from 80p/$1.25 – or bought from a mobile food stall. Compared to many other countries, even local mobile food stalls in Thailand are considered safe in terms of hygiene. As long as you are not too sensitive, you should definitely try one of the delicious dishes of this very special Thai 'fast food cuisine'.

Phang Nga Bay

It was an Englishman who made Phang Nga Bay, with its countless gigantic rocky islets, famous – none other than James Bond. Some of the scenes of the 1974 film *The Man With The Golden Gun* (starring Roger Moore as 007 and Christopher Lee as the villain Scaramanga) were shot on the island of Koh Ping Kan. From the mainland you can get to this small island with its characteristic rocks in about 45 minutes. Not far from here lies Koh Panyi, dominated by the small minaret of the Muslim fishermen's mosque. The village is partly on stilts, and boats can moor directly in front of one of its many restaurants.

In some places, the mainland shores of Phang Nga Bay are lined with mangroves, offering an unspoilt habitat to a rich variety of wildlife. Many of the caves of the rocky island, however, are surprisingly lively – bats roost there, packed tightly together in their hundreds.

One especially appealing way of experiencing the island world of Phang Nga Bay is by canoe. Large vessels with tourists and canoes on board come from the mainland for this reason, and once on site the visitors take to the canoes and head off between the rocks, into the hidden coves or through the bat caves.

Spirit Houses

Homes for all the good spirits – and bad

Just as Buddha is an institution in Thailand, the small houses on pedestals in front of (almost) every building are also part of everyday life in the country.

But what is it really all about? To the Thais, the entire world is full of spirits. They are in the woods, on the islands and of course also on the land where people live. And because the spirits were there first, they are not keen on the land changing ownership. So in order to keep a spirit from showing his anger toward the new residents, it gets its own house – highly visible from the entry door of the main building.

But what is a spirit house doing on that hill next to the main road?

Well – even a spirit needs a new home at some point. Maybe because it feels unhappy, or because it brings misfortune, or because its home looks unsightly. But because you never know whether or not a spirit still lives there, the old house is not disturbed, but rather transported to a hill in the woods. This is a place inhabited mostly by bad ghosts. To keep them from jumping into passing cars, people sound their horns loudly to keep them away. Sounding your horn is actually explicitly forbidden in this area – but you never know ...

Even spirits have standards – and if the property owner is wealthy, then this is reflected in the spirit house at the front door.

Frequent prayer is part of the life of the Thai monks.

Buddha, Temples and Incense

With the exception of the king, there is no-one in Thailand who is as revered as much as Siddhartha, the founder of Buddhism. Unlike in China, the Buddha in Thailand is portrayed as a thin man, and there is a temple or *wat* in every village, no matter how small. The largest on the island of Phuket is in Chalong. The more prosperous the setting of a monastery, the more impressive the details of the temple. Gold is lavishly used – although in modern times it tends to be a layer of gold paint over other material.

The monks who live in a temple are self-sufficient up to a point, while still partly supported by the willing population, but they will also ask for donations and gifts. The numerous daily prayers are part of everyday life for every Buddhist, and are the raison d'être for monks.

The exotic impression created by each and every temple is intensified by the scent of incense, which spreads its aroma throughout large temple complexes such as that at Wat Chalong.

Most commonly this comes from incense sticks, but there are also many other scents.

Also of interest are temples in rural areas or old temples like the one in the capital of Koh Lanta. In many places, you will see that the walls are old – as old as the desire to ward off those evil spirits who try to spread their mischief everywhere. Instead of a small spirit house, the temple is protected by the stern glares of the guards – who have been embedded in the walls since ancient times.

You will not see the world-famous temple dancers in the temples every night; you are more likely to catch them during a folklore evening at the hotel. In some temples, you can see large murals that show that the dancers definitely used to be around, with Buddha's blessing, and that they looked quite different from how they look today.

Some temples are closed on certain days, and you are advised to check before you make a visit. Generally, anyone interested in visiting a temple need not have any concerns. Buddhism is the most open and most peaceful religion imaginable – and for the European soul it is every bit as exotic as the holiday destination that is Thailand.

The temple dancers appear quite liberated in the murals of some temples.

Index

ASIA BOOKS

Published and distributed in Thailand by Asia Books Co., Ltd
No. 65/66, 65/70, 7th Floor, Chamnan Phenjati Business Center
Rama 9 Road, Huaykwang, Bangkok 10320, Thailand
Tel. (66) 2-715-9000; Fax: (66) 2-715-9197
E-mail: information@asiabooks.com; www.asiabooks.com

First published in the United Kingdom in 2012 by John Beaufoy Publishing,
11 Blenheim Court, 316 Woodstock Road, Oxford OX2 7NS, England
www.johnbeaufoy.com

10 9 8 7 6 5 4 3 2 1

ISBN 978-1-906780-73-9

Editor of German edition: Monika Weymann
Cover design, original layout and typesetting: Populärgrafik Stuttgart
Translation for English edition: Interlinguae Srl, Parma, Italy
English edition typeset by D & N Publishing, Baydon, Wiltshire

With 177 colour photos courtesy of the author, except for the photo of the Buddha
statue on page 9, Phuket
Photos of the diving bases, courtesy of the owners
Overview maps on pages 18, 26 and 106 by Wolfgang Lang
Site maps on pages 35, 67, 11, 130, 184 by William Smuts

Cover photos by Frank Schneider

Cover captions:
Front cover, left to right top row: Phang Nga Bay, Beach at Bang Niang, *King Cruiser*
wreck, Flower, Diver with sea fan corals.
left to right second row: Seahorse, Diver with leopard shark (*Boonsung* wreck),
Lionfish, Diver with whip corals, Diver with batfish.
main image: Diver with turtle.
Back cover: Blue-ring Angelfish (above); fan corals (below)

Printed and bound in Malaysia by Times Offset (M) Sdn. Bhd.